TEACHING WITHOUT STRESS

Harry Gray lectures at the University of Lancaster in school organization and management. He is author of several books on education including *The Management of Educational Institutions* and *Change and Management in Schools*.

Andrea Freeman is Principal Lecturer in Special Needs at Edge Hill College of Higher Education, Lancashire, and previously worked as an educational psychologist.

TEACHING
WITHOUT
STRESS

Harry Gray
and
Andrea Freeman

P·C·P
Paul Chapman
Publishing Ltd

First published 1988

Paul Chapman Publishing Ltd
London

British Library Cataloguing in Publication Data
Gray, Harry
    Teaching without stress.
    1. Teachers——Great Britain——Job stress
    I. Title   II. Freeman, Andrea
    371.1'04   LB2840.2

ISBN 1 85396 001 2

Typeset by Setrite Typesetters Ltd
Printed and bound by St Edmundsbury Press Ltd, Bury St Edmunds, Suffolk

CONTENTS

school • Why schools cause problems • Coping with freedom
• Success and failure of students • Understanding student
reactions • Problems of caring for students

FOREWORD

This book is intended to help teachers who are concerned about problems of stress either for themselves or colleagues and wish to understand how stress arises and how it might be dealt with. It is designed as an aid to reflection and a means of reducing the stress of being a teacher and working in schools.

Some readers may want an immediate answer to a problem of stress and for them reading it through from cover to cover will not provide help rapidly enough. So if answers are required to fairly specific points, the reader should either use the contents list at the beginning of each chapter or use the index to find mention of the various topics.

It is possible to skim the book by reading only the sections that are indented and placed within boxes. This provides a speedy overview of what the book is about.

The book is written within a framework of organization theory in that it links the responses of individuals to the structures of organizations. The intention is to provide an intellectual framework for working out and understanding how each of us can best cope with stress for ourselves.

Harry Gray

Andrea Freeman

1
THE NATURE OF STRESS AND THE MECHANICS OF COPING

● First steps in coping ● Why schools are stressful ● Definitions of terms used ●, Stress resulting from role ● A basic technique for coping with stress ● What goes wrong in school? ● Understanding yourself and stress

FIRST STEPS IN COPING

Reflection

The purpose of this book is to help you to understand the causes of stress in schools and how they may be dealt with. In writing the book we have made the underlying assumption that you are able to take positive action to cope better yourself and to help others to cope better. We hope that even just reading it quickly will be an enjoyable and rewarding experience.

The first step in coping is reflection

The first stage in dealing with a problem is to think about it. You probably cannot do this while you are in the middle of it so you will need to take time out to think about it — that is to reflect on what you think is happening and why you think you are reacting as you are.

Reflection is by itself a way of dealing with problems and usually the first stage of successful coping. We can reflect at two levels and both are necessary if reflection is to be really helpful.

One level of reflection is the intellectual one of understanding: of making sense of situations and our part in them by developing concepts that help us to find explanations to our satisfaction, and of comprehending what is going on and our part in events that affect us.

The other level is emotional: coming to understand the feelings we have about our experiences, accepting the personal nature of these feelings and finding the best ways of dealing with them.

These two aspects of reflection are mirrored in two other aspects of dealing with stress — solving problems and keeping emotions under control. Both go hand in hand and need to be dealt with alongside each other since though keeping calm may be a good thing it does not in the long run work to control stress unless some problem-solving has also been accomplished.

The basic perspective

We have written the book from perspectives that have developed through our experience as teachers and as people who have worked with teachers in a variety of contexts. Of course, our experience of education will be different from anyone else's but, as the focus is schools and working in schools, we are optimistic that we will have many experiences in common with others who have been or are still in schools.

WHY SCHOOLS ARE STRESSFUL

Schools as organizations

The first step to understanding how schools contribute to stress is to recognize that schools function in much the same way as other forms of organization.

All forms of organization are potential causes of stress simply because other people's needs and wishes impinge on us and have to be taken into consideration whether we like it or not.

People seldom feel stressed on their own; there is usually someone else feeling the same way. If you can seek that person out there will be someone to share your concerns with.

Individuality

The second step to understanding how schools cause us to be stressed is to acknowledge as perfectly legitimate the variety and extent of individuality in colleagues as well as students — let alone governors, inspectors, parents and councillors.

Organizationally schools tend not to like individual differences very much to the extent of creating considerable problems not only for specific people but for groups and consequently the whole organization itself. People respond to organizational situations in a wide variety of ways and we need to be tolerant of other people's differences. We need to identify our levels and areas of tolerance if we are to prevent ourselves from suffering stress.

You might like to try to make a list of what you consider intolerable behaviour in the case of the following:

1. Colleagues.
2. Students.
3. Parents.

Share your ideas of what is intolerable behaviour with a colleague and note the differences. Try to find out why you each have a different list of items and why some items are the same.

Our framework for managing stress

The framework we use in this book will enable you to examine your own working situations more usefully and help you to understand the causes of your own stress and that of others. In turn, this will help you to develop better strategies for preventing stressful situations from getting the better of you and will enable you to manage your relationships with colleagues and students in such ways that you do not suffer unduly from stress. We have expressed this framework diagrammatically in Figure 1.

DEFINITIONS OF TERMS USED

Words associated with stress

There are a number of words we shall use again and again, so we will provide some definitions at this point. Because the words are widely used there will be variations in meaning for different people and also different emphases and connotations. All of the words have both a personal and an organizational dimension and we need to remember that each of us perceives the same organization differently with the result that we respond differently – what delights one person may displease another; what is comfortable to one is irritating to another; and so on.

Stress

Stress is the key word in the book and it may also be the most confusing because it is used so loosely in ordinary conversation. Usually it is considered to be something unpleasant and to have its origin outside the individual; it is believed to be a pressure that is disagreeable or unacceptable.

> We do not see stress as always unpleasant but rather as a feeling state in response to something that is in an individual's environment and which may not have the same effect on other people. We identify this feeling state for ourselves.

Of itself, stress is neither good nor bad but it depends on how it is experienced. Stress can be stimulating or energizing, in which case it is positive and beneficial, or it can be the cause of feelings of anxiety, distress or discomfort; here it is a negative and harmful condition.

Because we all experience situations differently, the various effects that are experienced by individuals within the school may be acknowledged differently either as personal stress or as demands which create excitement, greater interest and more job satisfaction.

> Clarify in your own mind what circumstances or perceived pressures in your own school cause you to be
>
> 1. pleased and excited;
> 2. dejected and depressed.

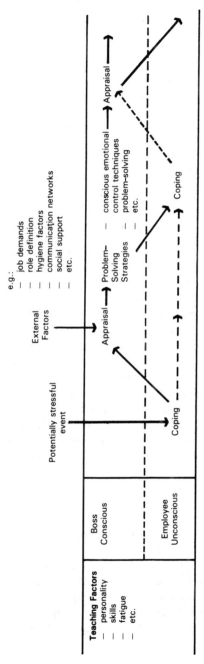

Figure 1 Framework for managing stress

> What demands are challenging and which are sources of stress for
> you? How do you account for these states and what do you do to
> bring them about or to cope with them when they arrive?

Some people are in a permanent state of some distress in schools — a
continual low level of stress — but it never becomes significant enough for
them to react badly against the system. But most people experience
significant stress from time to time and have to find ways of dealing with
it. When personal stress becomes too great, an individual may move into
a state of crisis which requires some resolution before they can return to
normal. A high level of stress may be associated with anxiety, which can
take many and various forms.

Anxiety

Anxiety is sometimes used as a technical term by medical practitioners,
psychologists and so on but it is also a well-understood common sense
term. It is used to describe the emotional reaction to an event which leads
us to divert our energies to coping with ourselves in some way; in other
words, we become preoccupied by our own feelings and unable to direct
our attention to external events.

Anxiety is a negative state that includes the feelings of tension, ap-
prehension and worry. In extreme cases, there are physical signs that
accompany the emotional turmoil, although these may be considerably
less significant for some individuals. These manifestations include rapid
and shallow breathing, increased heart rate, sweating, dryness of the
mouth, nausea, insomnia, trembling, restlessness, feelings of weakness
and inability to concentrate. Sometimes an individual will acknowledge
and accept these indications as signs of stress but in some cases, as with
chronic depression, the significance of the symptoms is denied.

Depression

Depression is a mood or state of mind in which we feel in low spirits,
lacking in energy, hopeless, perhaps useless and that life is particularly
unfair to us. When we are depressed we do not expect things to get better
and might even try to make them worse. We direct our bad feelings
towards ourselves and see ourselves as being blameworthy, ineffective, a
failure and disappointment. Everyone becomes depressed from time to
time and some people are in a general state of depression for weeks,

months or even years. But depressions usually lift and there are a number of techniques for helping us through them.

We need to remember that depression is something entirely in our own mind and is not a feature of whatever we are depressed about. We may feel that the school is depressing but the feeling is our own and that means there is a way out of it.

Depression and the anxiety that often accompanies it are probably much commoner in schools as an experience of both teachers and students than is generally recognized. For example, teachers may identify children as being difficult or impulsive rather than as under stress and feeling anxious. Or a teacher may be perceived as stern and without a sense of humour rather than as suffering from anxiety.

Collective anxiety

One effect of organizational stress is anxiety and whole groups such as a class or school staff may exhibit a variety of anxious behaviours, each member showing different ones. Anxiety can, of course, be a response to what is considered organizationally desirable or healthy, since individuals may not share the collective mythology of what is organizationally desirable. (Perhaps formal examinations fall into this category – though thought generally desirable they nevertheless create particular anxieties.)

Breakdown

At the extreme end of the continuum of anxiety and failure to cope is the 'breakdown'. This can be viewed as an emotional crisis and represents a point when people can be enabled to grow and learn better coping skills. After a breakdown we may well have a better understanding of ourselves and be able to see what other people like about us whereas before we could only see ourselves as being unable to cope adequately with the situation we faced.

> Some people use the idea of a 'nervous breakdown' as a means of coping better. By declaring that they are nearing a nervous breakdown they solicit support from their colleagues or family and this helps them to survive what might otherwise have been a very difficult time. Many of us have coping devices like this. Can you think of ways in which some of your colleagues cope best?

Burnout

Burnout is a concept related to breakdown and describes a form of stress which is usually considered to be at the opposite extreme to tedium. Burnout arises from too many demands being made that are of a personal emotional nature while tedium arises from unstimulating work which has little social or emotional meaning for us. It has been found that among social workers and teachers, it is usually the most idealistic and committed who 'burn out' first.

To counteract burnout teachers distance themselves from their students and their job so as not to become too deeply involved with people or school activities. This distancing is thought to enable the individual teacher to recoup their emotional resources and to cope better with the future but is, in fact, counter-productive. An individual who can separate personal life from business life will be more likely to cope with organizational stress than one who blends both personal life and private life into one — like many dedicated school teachers but such separation must not be at the expense of commitment. Burnout is both an organizational problem and a personal one because it happens to real people not just occupants of a role.

To check out on whether burnout could be a possibility for yourself, you should look at:

How long do you spend at school?
How many school colleagues are part of your social life?
How long do you spend on preparation in the evenings?
How many out-of-school activities do you engage in?
What you do during the school holidays?
Do you just work harder if you feel stressed?

STRESS RESULTING FROM ROLE

Roles

A good way of explaining stress in organizations is through role theory. Organizational role theory is a way of explaining how people relate to one another in organizations, in terms of the relationships that develop. Organizations consist of people who hold 'positions' and the organization works through the people who occupy the positions. They do this in ways that are unique to themselves and not as stereotypes, though there is

often the general expectation that people should behave 'impersonally' —
hardly a reasonable expectation.

The positions are, of course, themselves neutral; they are merely titles
and have no character until someone occupies them when they become
very individual. Thus roles are both self-created and subject to expectations
of those who are not role-holders. Problems arise when the role-holder
behaves differently from the way other members of the organization
expect them to behave. For example, a year tutor occupies a position
labelled *year tutor* which may have an official job description, but the
tutors will determine for themselves largely how to do the job and this
may well be in such a way as to confound the expectations of some
colleagues.

Role expectations of different people can never fully coincide so the
consequence is that there is always a potential area of stress around
people's roles in schools. We shall look at the effects of role expectations
at various points in this book because it is central to explaining the
problems we have with one another in almost every aspect of school
organization.

One thing is clear, no one has a correct definition of role, even the
role-holder. Tolerance of variations can be quite low in some circumstances and exceedingly high in others, according to how individuals
experience the particular characteristics of a given school.

Write down what you hope most of your colleagues will expect of
you as a colleague. Can you decide which ones you find most
difficult to live up to?

Sit down with a group of colleagues and discuss what your expectations of a particular role (e.g. deputy head) are.

All schools cause stress

It will be clear from what we have already said that stress can be expected
in all school organizations. Stress is a direct consequence of any kind of
organization and therefore everyone can be expected to show some signs
of being affected by it from time to time. By definition, organizations are
restricting and limiting because they co-ordinate and regulate behaviour
in some systematic way. Some people have a very sanguine view of
organization seeing it as invariably benign but there are good reasons for
not taking it for granted that any form of organization will suit all its
members, at least not all of the time.

When we are in a good relationship with our colleagues, we may be less likely to notice their problems. Good managers are always on the look out for signs of stress and have techniques for dealing with it constructively. All schools would function more effectively if there were a higher level of awareness (not just by senior staff but by everyone) that stress is a major factor in organizational behaviour. Good member relationships, high morale, and high productivity are possible only when the adverse effects of stress are minimized.

It is paradoxical that schools only too often show little concern for the effects of stress on both teachers and students even though they might be considered to be essentially client-centred institutions and therefore could be expected to have as a major concern the emotional well-being of their members.

Conflict

Because people are different from one another and perceive the organization(s) to which they belong differently, organizations are arenas of potential conflict, and eventually real conflict. Conflict resolution is the process by which differences are resolved; there can be no resolution of differences without conflict, though it may proceed no further than confrontation in a badly managed institution. Conflict is an essential element in the dynamics of organization; it is of the nature of organization to hold in tension the many possibilities open to its members and in making choices there is the inevitability of conflict.

Many teachers are afraid of conflict because they misunderstand it and think of it as fighting or destructiveness (which it may be on occasion). Yet conflict is often essential to the process whereby people come to agreement — though this may be by consensus, acceptance, collusion or accommodation. Schools like other organizations must work through the conflicts that arise in them and the sooner and more fully they are resolved the better for all concerned since the consequences are always increased personal stress.

Unresolved conflicts lead to fights and bitterness — alienation, withdrawal, rebellion, aggression and so on. For many people simply trying to avoid conflict is stressful and often more so than facing up to it — certainly it lasts longer. Many teachers may seek to avoid conflict among their colleagues by ignoring it, but in so doing they merely postpone the inevitable. Because much conflict occurs in working groups it is never enough just to talk problems through with key — or the most markedly stressed — individuals alone. Everyone involved should be included in the reconciliation process.

The importance of self-knowledge

Perhaps the most important concept to bear in mind when considering how to cope with stress in schools is that self-knowledge is more important than theories. Although senior staff — heads, deputies, heads of department, etc. — need to know how their actions affect others and how they themselves may improve the nature of organizational stresses, everyone (teachers and students) is a 'subjective' member of the school organization and it is critically important for each of us to understand ourself in the position we hold.

Most pressures that we feel in schools arise as a consequence of the kind of person we are rather than things that are done to us. We all need better self-knowledge, greater self-insight, so that we can initiate changes in our own behaviour that will improve not only our own situation but that of our colleagues.

A BASIC TECHNIQUE FOR COPING WITH STRESS

How to cope with stress

To understand how to cope with stress it is necessary to understand the nature of stress at the personal level. The fundamental feature of stress is *appraisal*, which means the process whereby we analyse a situation in which we perceive a threat to ourselves. It is essential to remember when talking about causes of stress that stress is always personally defined and that there is nothing that can be called a form of stress or a cause of stress (a *stressor*) in general since there will always be someone for whom that potential cause (stressor) is not appraised as a stressor.

A situation which causes one person stress will be the source of challenge and excitement to another. Compare the sources of stress that you experience with those of a colleague much less or much more experienced in teaching than yourself. What are the differences that you notice?

Appraisal

Because stress is differently caused for everyone, its nature, causes and manifestations are not universal. But by accepting the personal nature of stress we can understand the process through the concept of appraisal.

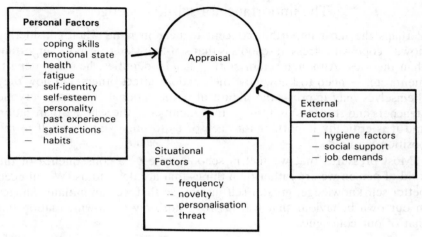

Figure 2 Aspects of self-appraisal

Appraisal works as the process by which we decide whether or not we feel stressed; we make our own decision that we are stressed by 'appraising' the cirumstances in the light of our previous experience. To make the decision we take into account a range of experiences, some of which relate to us and some to other people, and accounts and reports of which we are aware. This is illustrated in Figure 2. Each of the three appraisal areas shown in Figure 2 – personal, situational and external – will be considered briefly to clarify the model illustrating how self-help can be assisted.

WHAT GOES WRONG IN SCHOOL?

Performance

Sometimes teachers see the teaching role as an acting, or performing, activity requiring a largely passive audience. Most classroom teaching involves 'performance' in that a teacher has to work with a group of people in a leadership role and much of what happens in the classroom will depend on their initiative and management; the students are passive only so that they might become involved as soon as it is appropriate for them to do so.

Factors that will be relevant at the time of appraisal will be the energy level, or level of fatigue, general state of health and sense of satisfaction with the job. Tired people tend to be less effective than wide-awake ones. There are often levels of fatigue of which we are not particularly aware, yet any level of fatigue will contribute to the experience of stress. Similarly, our general state of health can dramatically affect us. Those infections which raise our temperature also affect how we think and feel and may also change our awareness of reality. Some illnesses affect other aspects, for example, physical co-ordination, and it is often invisible illnesses that cause most problems. A broken leg is obvious and people feel and express sympathy, but someone who is just feeling under the weather as they succumb to influenza may be treated quite unsympathetically.

On the other hand, if we feel fit and healthy we feel more able to tackle problems, face stressful situations and exude a feeling of *bonhomie*. Feelings of dissatisfaction with the job can change our appraisal of situations by its power to change positive aspects into negative ones. If we are feeling satisfied, we tend to value ourself more highly and appraise our work more positively. But if we are feeling dissatisfied with our job our perceptions will take a negative view.

For example, a teacher who is asked to organize a Christmas show will respond according to their basic disposition. If they feel satisfied with their job this may be seen as a welcome challenge, as a beneficial aspect of the job, as a reward or a recognition of competence. But teachers who feel negatively about their job, for whatever reasons, may see the request as extra work, a thankless task, an imposition, a drag on private time, a lot of unnecessary hassle. Yet both teachers might be as effective as one another in the normal day-to-day running of the school.

A more significant factor, however, is past experience. Much learning involves 'one trial learning' – which is learning by our mistakes. We try something once and if we like the experience we will be prepared to do it again but if it proves unpleasant we may be unwilling to try again. We are often like that with food. Someone offers us a mango for the first time and we dislike the taste so we avoid mangoes ever after. But then one day a close friend whose cooking we admire offers us a dish that tastes quite delicious but does not reveal what is in it. After we have expressed enjoyment they reveal that it is a mango dish. We express surprise, re-evaluate our opinion of mangoes and from then onwards enjoy the fruit whenever it is available.

It is just the same with social situations. We identify situations as being unpleasant or pleasant by virtue of certain key characteristics. But because human situations are so complex, we may misread the indicators for their significance and create a stressful situation based on precedent that would not otherwise be stressful for us. On the other hand we may misread stressful situations and sail through them untouched by anxiety. We can become oversensitive to some kinds of situation that we have found stressful and create them where they do not actually exist.

Children are experts at finding our weak spots and can detect our sensitivity very easily, often without really knowing it. Older students can be quite deliberate in doing those things that upset a teacher they dislike. Teachers who are sensitive of their 'performance' may react emotionally instead of rationally to adverse behaviour from their students, because they are too sensitive to their own success or failure. But with practice we can learn to evaluate our response to a situation so that the emotional element in our responses is separated from the rational.

Conscious and deliberate appraisal allows us to interrupt the automatic response and consider positive actions for better coping.

Changing our view of events

Our past experience will not only affect our interpretation of events but also our judgement about how we feel about them and what we ought to do. Sometimes a new situation can be stressful or very exciting simply because we have had no prior experience of it. Indeed many people appear to have hobbies which essentially produce higher adrenalin levels for enjoyment; for example hang-gliding or parachute-jumping are presumably more exciting than the weekly job for the people who engage in these sports. The enjoyment is in the fear and exhilaration not the comfort and security! But over time the effects may wear off and the enjoyment may be less because there is less fear, with a consequence that the sportsman looks for even more dangerous ways of performing his activity.

One way of reappraising a novel and stressful situation is to think of it as exciting and challenging rather than as frightening. In this way facing a new or difficult class can be appraised differently from the previous stressful situation.

Using past experience

So far we have considered past experience in terms of 'one trial learning', oversensitivity and novelty — all of which in some circumstances might be unhelpful. Past experience should always be considered positively because it includes learning and that should mean it is easier not to make the same kind of mistake again. We should be able to recognize stressful situations in the making and 'defuse' them before they get out of hand.

Teachers are usually very good at recognizing some signs from a class that there is going to be trouble and take avoiding action appropriately. They may claim that this is intuitive but it is informed and experienced intuition. Additionally, past experience enables us to make choices from a range of experiences or actions; experience tell us that there are no single 'right' ways of doing things but there are always better ways and worse ways.

For example, if a minor conflict arises in a classroom between two pupils there will be a number of different tactics available ranging from totally ignoring the incident to authoritarian suppression. The choices teachers make will depend on their experience of tactics that have proved successful or otherwise in the past and the kinds of long- and short-term consequences, such as improved or worsened relationships with certain students.

Developing good habits

Past experience also leads to the development of habits. In human relation-ships we often use short cuts to prevent overloading our decision-making capacity. This applies when we develop stereotypes as a means of dealing with people; we label them and that saves us the trouble of having to deal with them in a special way.

Underachieving children are a case in point. Some teachers prepare themselves for coping with them by using a stereotype such as 'all remedial children are poorly dressed, are neglected by their parents, are of low stature, cannot concentrate for long, have a chip on their shoulder, etc.'. Following on from the stereotype come set routines for dealing with the stereotyped person. Ordinary life is full of these routines and rituals because they are the best way of coping with the large number of social encounters we engage in each day. They can be very defensive and counter-productive.

Habits and rituals

Sometimes we cannot actually hear what someone is saying to us because we have established already what they will say and decided to ignore it. Sometimes rituals are a way of reinforcing a relationship because we go through a sequence of responses that are familiar to both parties and gives a sense of security in the relationship. There is a common ritual with children who have been asked to do something. They question first 'Why should I?' The adult responds 'Because I would like you to because....'. The child questions again and the adult reasons again, perhaps asserting authority in some desperation for the job to be done. By delaying the start of the task the child has gained some time, perhaps managed to finish something enjoyable like watching the TV, enjoyed the attention of an adult, and taken some responsibility for doing the job anyway.

Many habitual relationships like this occur in school. Some are specific to an individual student, some common to all the students in an age group or class. In appraising ourselves with regard to a particular stressor we need to examine the habitual aspects of behaviour to see if there is anything that happens automatically and that we can prevent.

UNDERSTANDING YOURSELF AND STRESS

Consistent personality

We need, too, to be aware of our personality and the way the kind of person we are determines our responses and reactions. In this regard we can take a common sense view of personality while remembering that the term has a specialized usage among pyschologists. We know that we tend to behave differently in different situations and with different people. Some people are more anxious than others, more self-confident, more placid and so on. Whatever the origin of these personality characteristics they tend towards consistency and continuity so that our interpretations of events and our own behaviour will be influenced by them.

For example, if we are generally phlegmatic we are not likely to be easily stressed. If we are self-centred, we will be keenly stressed by events that seem to threaten us. It is important for each of us to be as clear as possible about the kind of person we are and what our strongest characteristics are. If we do not have self-awareness of this kind we shall never be able to control our responses to the world we live and work in.

Emotional colouring

Our emotional state will take its colouring from the kind of person we are, from our personality, as well as from what happens to us. Someone in love will respond differently to the loved one than to a friend. Different people are capable of different kinds of love, perhaps different levels.

Our emotional state may vary for no apparent reason. We may feel energetic and cheerful one minute and sad and downcast another, and when asked why this has happened we may be lost for an explanation. Our unaccountable moods will influence our interpretation of events and it may differ from place to place over a short timespan.

Being fed up

One of the commonest feelings is that of feeling *fed up*. It is a very general term with no precise meaning but used to imply a general feeling of malaise. We can be fed up in a lot of different ways but the term is interesting just because it is another of those catch-all words used to refer to feelings and emotions. Whatever the specific nature of being fed up it has an effect over a wide range of experiences; a whole day can be put out of joint by this one disposition and we will tend to act with irritation to things that would not normally upset us.

Often being fed up is a form of mild depression in which case we tend towards self-blame, but in its more severe forms we see other people as blameworthy and curse and criticize all and sundry round us. In the classroom a fed-up teacher might become very sensitive to trivial matters of disobedience, talking loudly or even the normal level of activity in the classroom.

It is often difficult for us to draw ourselves out of a black mood. But by turning attention outward towards the students and looking for positive reactions from them, a situation of general despondency can be gradually enlivened by appreciative responses; we just begin to look for them.

Identity and self-esteem

Personality is basically a matter of self-identity and self-esteem. They are the bases on which judgements are made not only about ourselves but about other people since we normally judge others with regard to our view of ourselves. If we perceive threats to our self-esteem − perhaps a class of students is not doing so well as a comparable class and we assume it must be our fault − we enter into a period of stress because something quite fundamental to ourselves is at risk − we feel inadequate and incompetent.

An authoritarian teacher whose authority is publicly challenged by a pupil will suffer more from loss of face than a teacher who is more easy going with students. Some teachers would suffer no loss of face at all if they were cheeked by a pupil because they would understand such behaviour as being a consequence of how students feel about themselves rather than as a comment upon the teacher's abilities.

Satisfactory appraisal involves an assessment of not only the material circumstances, including the perceptions of others of the situation, but your view of yourself. We need to remember that we are not the only actor in a situation and that others are responding at the very same time as we are; they too have their perceptions and reactions.

It is usual for us simply to guess at the reactions of others and to organize our responses accordingly. But we may well be mistaken and have completely misinterpreted them, even when they are from someone we know well. Self-knowledge extends to an awareness of the kinds of assumption we make about other people and how we build them up into scenarios.

We have all been in the situation when we have to face an uncomfortable interview when we fear we are going to be reprimanded. We usually rehearse what is going to happen and the behaviour of the other person, running through lengthy conversations in which we manage to cope successfully or even come out as winner. Of course, the real event is not as we imagine it but sometimes we are better at prediction than others.

Since we do sometimes guess correctly, it is worth trying to find out why sometimes we are right while at other times we predict quite wrongly. Achieving accuracy is perhaps more difficult than it sounds since interpersonal communications are very complex and fraught with misunderstandings which usually arise from mistakes of interpretation of signals. Even with people whom we know well, we still make mistakes and may wrongly understand a tone of voice or a raised eyebrow. Sometimes this does not matter but at other times it can lead to problems. We should always try to confirm an interpretation before coming to a conclusion.

Feedback and coping

This bring us perhaps to the most important aspect of coping skills — using feedback effectively. We appraise situations to be stressful because we do not have the skills to cope. When considering our skills, talents, weaknesses and characteristics we can make mistakes through relying on but misinterpreting feedback from others. If we have been told that we are efficient or competent or a good teacher, but on insufficient evidence, we may incorporate this information into our view of ourselves. This can lead to considerable problems of evaluation when we are in crisis situations. But if we have a critical view of ourselves we will be less influenced by gratuitous opinions.

Sometimes, the evaluations others share with us of ourselves are much more critical and if we have a low self-esteem we will take too much notice of others' views. Sadly, many more people suffer from being put down than being overpraised and many have their sense of inadequacy and helplessness reinforced rather than queried. People with low self-esteem and a sense of personal helplessness find coping with a wide range of circumstances very difficult and teachers who are like this will perceive many threats of all kinds from students who are perfectly reasonable in their behaviour.

> However stressful a situation you find yourself in, it is worth making time to consider how reasonable your reactions are. If you judge your behaviour as unreasonable, you have the chance to change it by re-evaluating it.

Two other factors to be considered are situational and external. We do not normally feel stressed without some event occurring which causes it. Sometimes we may have psychological reactions which resemble feelings of stress and we ask ourselves why we feel this way. This has been found to occur with some forms of medication which act upon the central nervous system and also as an allergic reaction to certain foods and chemicals. But in general there is always a cause of stress in any event in which we have a part.

To cope with stress we therefore need to have some knowledge of factors relating to the situation. The impact of the causal event will relate to four dimensions: personalization, frequency, novelty and degree of threat. The degree of threat does not necessarily refer to physical stress but can refer to self-esteem, self-image, health, emotional state, etc.

Threat seems to depend partly on the level of personalization that is involved because if we perceive ourselves as marginal to a situation we will not be much affected by it. A child who acts violently towards us in a class will be perceived as a greater threat if we believe we are the sole target of their anger than if we believe they are using us as a target representative of an animosity really directed at the school.

Predictability

The frequency with which events occur and whether they are predictable are also part of our appraisal of stress. If events happen regularly but we are unable to avoid them or deal with them, our level of stress will be heightened.

An example in school is the difficult class that you have to teach each day; your anxiety level rises as the time for the class gets nearer, perhaps immediately preceded by a high adrenalin level as you prepare to meet the fray. If you do not handle the class as well as is acceptable to you, you will tend to feel worse the next time. The fact that you are anxious about meeting the class may communicate itself to the students, who may respond by fulfilling your worst expectations. At least the regular class has the merit of predictability, and you can develop methods of coping in readiness each time.

Events, however, that are unpredictable may have a greater shock impact though we may be unaware of the extent of our coping while things are going on. If, however, we are subject to a series of unpredictable events we may suffer to the point of withdrawal. Pupils whose behaviour is predictably bad are really less of a problem than those who behave badly without a pattern. It is these latter students who are excluded from mainstream schools and are sent to schools for the 'maladjusted'.

Among external factors are what are sometimes called 'hygiene' factors or those associated with general working conditions. They tend not to be primary causes of stress for teachers but rather exacerbate the situation which has other causes. When pupils misbehave and working conditions are poor, resources limited, rooms are underheated, etc., the primary cause of stress is pupil behaviour, but teachers add these other factors to their perception of causes and speak of them as if they were separate causes instead of the secondary ones they really are.

Social support

Social support is of great importance in coping with stress. Teachers spend a good deal of their time alone with their students and may have little to do with their colleagues except for quite superficial and casual relations. The amount of social support available, however, can make all the difference between stress and euphoria; talking things over and sharing experiences are essential to continued coping. Social support is one of the best ways of preventing potentially stressful events making us feel stressed.

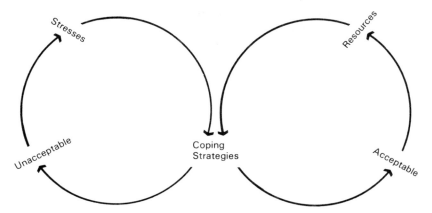

Figure 3 The relationship between stress, resources and coping

It is quite likely that one reason teachers 'talk so much shop' — and often talk about students to people who have never met them — is that they have a great deal of anxiety about how effective they are in the classroom. The classroom is a place no other adult shares with them so there can be no talking out of experiences with someone who was actually there.

The specific demands of a teacher's job are another element in the picture. It is difficult to determine exactly what the demands of a teacher's job are; so much is taken for granted as arising out of the situation. No two classes make quite the same demands or give the same returns. If teachers feel a little anxious about their performance or under-rewarded for what they are doing, they may find an expressed requirement from the head (or even from his or her analysis of class needs) as just too much. In this case the stress arises from the teachers having already predetermined that stress will arise at a certain point and they may even have been preparing psychologically (that is, subconsciously) for it because there is now a justification for failure or breakdown. Figure 3 provides a summary of the relationship between stress, resources and coping.

The definition of coping strategies as good or not can only be made in terms of the effects afterwards. To some extent this will depend on the frequency with which a strategy is used and whether use leads to an increase in resources. If a strategy permits coping but with negative consequences it can hardly be said to be a good strategy. Resigning from or leaving an organization is a good coping strategy if it allows one to move into a situation which is now free from stress, but if one is as stressed afterwards as before it is clearly unsuccessful. Repeatedly resigning with the same undesirable effects is not a good coping strategy but is instead a means of inducing stress.

2
STRESS AND THE
TEACHING PROFESSION

● Facing public criticism ● Dealing with value conflicts ● Autonomy in the classroom ● Conflicting objectives in school and classroom ● Problems of authority ● Causing your own stress ● Obsession with trivia ● Handling discipline ● Maintaining control

FACING PUBLIC CRITICISM
The problems of a profession

One of the problems of professions is that the context in which they are performed is never entirely clear or simple. It is, for instance, impossible to do the job of a teacher and please everyone with whom you come into contact because everyone expects something different of you. Part of the problem is that professions define themselves in their own terms rather than by doing what the customer wants of them. It may be arguable whether teaching is a true profession but it certainly has many of the characteristics of one even if it lacks the legal and administrative aspects (such as regulation of entry) of a true profession and if it is lacking in a sense of mystique. Lawyers and doctors can call on their peers to validate their actions with some certainty of support, but for teachers there is usually no such back up and a teacher can often feel let down by colleagues who may not rally round as much as is needed.

Perhaps the best way of thinking about yourself as a professional is to think of yourself as someone who is there to help rather than to uphold professional standards. Some people confuse themselves by trying to do what they think is 'professionally' correct instead of what their clients need them to do.

List for yourself five ways in which you are generally helpful to students.

Facing public criticism

Teachers often feel as if they are being got at when they meet other people at parties and gatherings. As soon as you say you're a teacher some people will take a swipe at teachers, schools and education in general and the criticism will be so broad and generalized that it is difficult to answer. In any case, it always appears that everyone knows what a teacher ought to do and members of the general public are not at all reticent in applying memories of schooldays to current educational problems. Not only is teaching open to so many outside interpretations but internally there are many ambiguities and uncertainties that cannot but lead to a certain amount of occupational stress.

When someone makes an attack on the teaching profession which you find yourself taking personally and wanting to defend, it is a good idea to agree with what is said and let the speaker continue with what they want to say. Nothing is gained by reacting sharply but after they have said their say you can add gently, 'Well, that's one way of thinking about it, I suppose.'

Then say more only when you have calmed down.

Education and schooling

Part of the problem of talking with people about education lies in the difficulty of defining the word *education* and its common confusion with *schooling*. In normal conversation people do not define their terms very carefully and in many conversations there is much talking at cross purposes. Education is a catch-all word that can soon lead to considerable fogginess of thinking. Most of the public rhetoric about education, training and schooling is characterized by such fogginess and a great deal of woolly argument that often makes it very difficult for professional educators — like teachers — to argue coherently because the focus of the argument keeps changing. This leads to confusion for teachers themselves and no little exasperation at not being able to explain matters.

> When an individual is under stress — such as from an unexpected 'attack' on schools or whatever — arguing about principles and ideas will be unsuccessful because the problem of the accuser lies at a deeper level of experience than discussion can reach.
>
> There will be some hurt arising from past experience and only a sympathetic hearing will allow the anger or frustration to be talked out.
>
> In any dispute or argument, try to get your opponent to define their terms. Define your terms, too, as soon as you are aware that an argument is evolving.

DEALING WITH VALUE CONFLICTS

Organization and values

In schools where the teachers share a common value system there will be a high degree of harmony and mutual support, but where there are different personal values there will sooner or later be a conflict in one form or another. A teacher's whole approach to teaching is a consequence of a personal philosophy. Many conflicts become elevated to the level of political gaming because they originate in ideological standpoints that are not openly acknowledged; most factionalism and some trade unionism arise from this base.

> Our educational values are personal and therefore may not be shared by colleagues. We should be careful not to force our expectations on others. A great deal of unhappiness is experienced by teachers and heads who expect others to think as they do. Trying to respect the views of others is more than just tolerance, it is a way of preventing personal stress.

Organizational values

Organizational values derive from the personal value systems of key members of the school who are also the most powerful. This will usually mean that the head sets the values, though in large schools there will be differences among departments particularly when these departments have a high profile or involve a large number of students and teachers. Key people impose their values on others because they set the standards required in relationships – not many assistant teachers tell the head how to behave!

Every so often we find ourselves in a school where we are unhappy because our personal values do not coincide sufficiently with others in the school or the dominant school values. Usually we do not recognize this is the reason for our unhappiness but look for an explanation that is more tangible. But often there are no tangible reasons why we are unhappy in a school; it is just that our ways of looking at things are so different that events are continually being interpreted differently and we feel increasingly alienated.

When we recognize that we are working in the wrong school environment and are quite clear of the reason being a clash of values, we really have no option but to look elsewhere for another job. This is perfectly acceptable because individuals cannot change organizations to any considerable degree.

But if you cannot seek a job elsewhere or while you are waiting to, concentrate on your own values in the classroom. One advantage of being a teacher is that you can do things in the classroom largely without interference. If the students respond well to you, you need have no other concern.

Values and choice

One of the remarkable things is that we should expect the value system of a school to be appropriate for everyone who is a member. One basic purpose of interviewing applicants for a job is to check out on both sides that a value match will be possible. It is unfortunate that many involved in recruitment do not recognize this. But at least most teachers have some choice in the matter; they actively seek new employment and make a calculated choice.

> To find out about the value system of a school, there are four leading questions you might ask at a job interview:
>
> What reward system does the school operate?
> What is the school's view of punishment?
> What is the school's view of the individual student?
> How do the teaching staff participate in decision-making?

For students, joining a school is more often than not a case of Hobson's choice, even if their parents visit a few schools before enrolling their offspring. Schools tend to overlook the confusion in which students find themselves when they move from one environment with its strong value system (the home, the family) into another which is equally (and perhaps more so) insistent on another system of values that may well be in conflict and which can apply severe sanctions in what must often seem an arbitrary way.

> Value conflicts lead to much unacknowledged stress among teachers and heads as well as students.

Climate and values

Although we have introduced the word *values*, schools tend not to use it in quite the way we have but use instead words such as *climate* and *ethos*; sociologists sometimes also use the word *culture*. They are all related concepts. Values, however, are essentially personal and are expressed in behaviour, attitudes, dispositions and perspectives. They are never neutral and always express or represent an opinion and a preference.

> Consider what matters to you most about being a teacher. Do you know how many of your colleagues feel the same way?

Climate is the consequence of individuals working things out together and bringing their different beliefs, etc. into a working relationship − or else failing to do this resulting in a general climate of conflict and bitterness. In some instances different values apply in different sections of the organization − the classroom as against the games field, for example.

Another good example is the change in values between lower and upper parts of a secondary school. A lower school may espouse caring, benevolent attitudes based on ideas of liberal education in a largely unstreamed teaching environment, while the upper school where there is often an expectation that students will be recalcitrant employs punitive and authoritarian methods, with teaching organized in streamed examination-orientated groups. The pupils experience a dissonance between the two and may find adjustment unnecessarily difficult, while teachers who have to teach in both sections may find themselves unable to cope adequately with two quite different professional demands or may feel threatened by older pupils if they never teach in the upper school.

Teachers who recognize the incompatibility between the two internal cultures may decide to opt for teaching in only one section of the school. Being true to one's own values is more important to our emotional well-being than courting the opinions of others.

The ethos of a school is much less tangible than some teachers imagine and is more likely to be what people believe it to be rather than a truly common and agreed experience. Descriptions of the ethos may simply be expressions of fantasy and so a problem in their own right. Teachers used to talk about 'the ethos of the grammar school' as if it were a substantive and common phenomenon, but ethos can only be an abstraction and a personal construct.

Value conflict and dissonance

We should not understimate the importance of value conflict or dissonance among teachers in schools. For one thing, there is the discrepancy between expressed values and experienced or practised values. Heads may claim to be supportive of colleagues whatever they do, but in practice they may come over as always taking the other side. (Even when one person has good intentions in what they do another may experience them as hurtful.)

One technique that some bosses adopt is always to take the side of their own superiors when there is the likelihood of a showdown. In so doing they undermine their good relationships with their colleagues by trying to distance themselves in such a way that they can take credit for what goes well, but dissociate themselves from matters when they go badly. By behaving in this way they feel they can always be right. But the consequence is that their colleagues feel scapegoated or let down and morale is lowered.

This kind of experience is not limited to teachers but will be ex
by students with some frequency; they will explain it by sayir
one rule for the teachers and one rule for them. For instance, stu~~
often complain that teachers never apologize for their mistakes while
students have to undergo public mortification for relatively minor offences.
Teachers need to examine carefully the differences in the way students
are treated as against the way teachers are. Older students especially do
not appreciate being treated as children any more than adults do.

> Teachers often become aware of being stressed when they come into
> conflict with students who insist that their behaviour is not wrong
> though the teacher insists that it is. The reason is often a clash of
> values; the teacher is expecting of the student different behaviour
> from what would be expected of an adult.
>
> In other words, one cause of stress for teachers is not realizing
> that they are unconsciously operating on two different sets of values.
> A simple question to ask is 'Would I ask a colleague to do this for
> me?'

AUTONOMY IN THE CLASSROOM

It is a commonly held view that once teachers close the classroom door
they can do more or less what they like. This is not entirely true, of
course, but there is a good deal of truth in it, and a consequence is that
head teachers have very little control over their colleagues when it comes
to actual classroom management and teaching styles, etc. This a double-
edged autonomy since teachers often feel isolated in their classrooms
even though they are safe from observation by their peers.

The performance aspect of teaching then takes on greater significance
and may be one of the major sources of personal stress for teachers, since
both performance and evaluation of performance vary according to so
many factors: subject taught, personality of teacher, age and development
of students, type of school, etc.

> In the classroom it is essential to gain the good will of the students.
> The key to this is gaining their respect, and to do this we must both
> respect ourselves and respect the students. Without respect there
> can be no class discipline or good order.

The isolate-teacher

Almost every school has at least one teacher who is an isolate, or 'ploughs a lone furrow'. In primary and other small schools the organizational consequences can be considerable. The isolate-teachers cause problems because they are happy not to relate to other colleagues. Isolates are often allowed to continue in their isolation and the staff group continues to feel incomplete and disconnected.

The cause of the problem is often that in schools decisions are often made by default rather than by a process of consensus. This means that there is not enough appropriate discussion before a decision is made so people feel that decisions have been taken over their heads. This alienates otherwise committed teachers and further isolates teachers who do not participate much anyway.

> In decision-making not everyone has to agree but at least they can agree to agree or accept. Participation in the process of discussion is much more important than being an actual decision-maker. Most people would rather let someone else decide, so long as they have been consulted about a matter.

Achieving good will

Lack of good will can undermine the philosophy and ethos of the school. For example, if the head of a primary school and most of the teaching staff welcome the participation of parents in the school and yet one teacher withdraws good will and does not co-operate, the whole scheme may be jeopardized. Such a person may be thought of as the weak link or the bad apple.

Both the head and the teacher have problems in this circumstance but they are quite different. The head has the problem of dealing with both co-operative staff and the non-cooperative one who may need very careful handling if the refusal situation is not to be made worse. The teachers who will not co-operate have problems within themselves which may be very difficult to get at and impossible to share. But it should not be assumed that anyone who takes negative and reactive action against colleagues is happy with what they are doing. A lot of personal and private unhappiness manifests itself in unpleasant public forms.

> To save ourselves from becoming angry with people who won't fall into line with what we want, we should think about how we ourselves feel when we are being coerced. Anger at other people is often the result of frustration with ourselves.

Commitment

We sometimes assume, when talking about schools in a general sense, that all the teachers on a school staff ought to have an energetic and positive view about their school. Teachers value their creativity and hard work highly, but there is no reason why teachers should be any different from any other group of workers; that means there are all shades of enthusiasm and commitment. The fact is that in every school everyone has some measure of dissociation otherwise work would be impossible. School is not the one and only consideration in life and if it were it would be so limiting that teachers would be too closed-minded to be of much use to their students.

> The best way to avoid the increasing pressures of the school is to keep the school at an emotional distance so that it does not absorb all our time and energies. Being over-committed is a distinct disservice to the school.

There are considerable pressures on teachers to do more than just teach. Traditionally teachers have been much involved in what have been somewhat incorrectly termed 'out of school activities' — since most of them took place in school even if outside normal classroom organization. But this expectation often goes beyond extra activity into expecting teachers to set a good example to their students — which sometimes appears to mean a perfect example. Surprisingly, most teachers do accept that they should provide some kind of model example to their students in their public life at least, but this puts them under some strain particularly when they live in the same area as their students.

> The difficulty in being a model teacher is that it is impossible to model for everyone; to try to be everyone's ideal is to put oneself under unbearable strain. Teachers who try to set too high an example will be pulled in so many directions that they cease to function properly or consistently in ordinary relationships.

You can't do everything

Teachers are likely to define their roles in terms of tasks that they perceive as legitimate to their role as teacher. It is commonplace to hear a teacher describe a particular task as 'It's not my job to...'. The missing words will change according to the age of the students and the school where the teacher works, but it is usually intended as a statement of professionalism and an attempt, albeit negatively expressed, to manage the all-embracing role by cutting it down to size.

The deputy head who claimed with relish that she was 'general dogsbody' in the school was also trying to show professionalism in her overinclusiveness even though to others the claim sounded like self-deprecation. But the actual effect of this view of herself was to increase her personal confusion about the nature of her job and herself as a teacher so that she became pulled apart as she tried to be all things to all people. Above all, she neglected to recognize her own personal needs and this reinforced her sense of personal inadequacy and made it difficult for her colleagues to relate to her in the way she needed.

The more rigid your job definition the more likely you are to be stressed by other people's demands on you since if you have to do what you do not consider to be your job such demands will be defined as stressful.

CONFLICTING OBJECTIVES
IN SCHOOL AND CLASSROOM

Objectives and purposes of schools

The matter of commitment and involvement relates to the matter of objectives. The current fashion is to require schools to state their objectives, publish them in a handbook for parents and state how they are to be achieved. On the face of it, this sounds a splendid idea but there are serious problems.

In the first place schools cannot have objectives because they are inanimate. Individuals may have objectives for themselves and agree on some common ones when they associate in an organization, but this only means that the organization becomes the vehicle for an amalgam of individual objectives. For this reason a school's objectives cannot be measured because they relate to individuals. Since we can never be clear about personal objectives and whether they are attainable (because they are bound up in a complexity of personal considerations) we cannot properly evaluate organizational objectives however broadly or precisely they are expressed.

> The problem with organizational objectives is that they reduce personal needs and objectives to an irrelevant generality. Consequently no one gets what they need and everyone becomes alienated in some measure.

However, it can be claimed that organizations serve purposes and that they exist to facilitate the attainment of personal objectives. This means that schools have to serve conflicting interests and they can do this only if they seek to deal with individuals as individuals and not abstractions.

How individuals set the objectives

The best way of dealing with the problem of objectives is to agree that the purpose of the school is to facilitate a certain broad range of activities and to claim this facilitative function as the organizational purpose. The difficulties then come only in dealing with unforeseen demands and outcomes. Individuals set themselves objectives in tune with their own value systems and this means they will exclude concerns that are either marginal to or outside their value system.

An important question, then, is whether the values are the organization's or the individual's. For example, a head might be opposed to gambling for personal reasons but is asked by some colleagues if they might hold a raffle for a charity. He may agree because he considers raffles harmless and the charity worthwhile. But then some sixth formers come to him and ask if they can organize a poker tournament for a similar charity. The head will probably refuse for the simple reason that poker is beyond his boundary of acceptable gambling. Yet for his students, poker may be one of the more innocuous forms of gambling. We cannot say that one of the objectives of the school is to promote raffles or that it is to discourage gambling, but either of these conclusions might be deduced from a general objective 'to develop initiative and social responsibility on the part of students'.

Schools and factories

Schools are neither like manufacturing organizations in that they do not have a material product nor like commerce are they simply service organizations. It is a mistake to think of schools as manufacturing plants though they have been so described by some educationists. Schools do not process or convert raw material into standard products, which is what manufacturing industry does, and to perceive them as such betrays a dangerous view not only of schools but of the students in them. If students are thought of as inanimate substances to be moulded and shaped then there are some inevitable problems for both teachers and students.

Education, in whatever form of schooling it may occur, is essentially a matter of personal relationships at a very high level of intimacy. Some teachers will find this easier to do in a small class while others will be more comfortable in a large class. In all possibility large classes are to be preferred (other matters like teacher competence and class management skills being equal) because the effect of teacher behaviour will be dissipated more widely and the more stress-creating behaviours will be weakened. This does not mean that the students will learn less, because a well-managed class will for the most part look after itself and the requests for help from individual students will be more task-related.

Schools should relate group and class size to the needs of both teachers and students. Uniform class size may cause more problems than it solves, creating personal problems rather than administrative ones.

Both teachers and students have different tolerances and needs for intimacy. Both teachers and students may become distressed if the right level of intimacy is not achieved.

PROBLEMS OF AUTHORITY

Authority in the classroom

As soon as we talk about class management and teacher behaviour in the school we raise the question of authority. However they earn it, teachers always hold a position of authority in the classroom even if it rapidly diminishes once they are away from the school. Classroom authority depends on the way the class is managed and the extent to which the students feel their needs are being attended to. If they feel that they matter to the teacher they will forgive a good deal but if they feel they are being used for the teacher's personal ends they will rebel in some way.

Authority in the classroom falls to the teacher as the consequence of teacher behaviour; it is not a preordained state in which the teacher enters the classroom — teachers have to earn authority, they cannot just assume it.

Teachers may come under stress when they believe they have more authority than their students accord them or, perhaps surprisingly, when they believe they have less than they attribute to them. It is a question of the sense of reality of each teacher; where this is poor they may be deluded into behaviour that increases confrontation or withdrawal by students, both of which are stressful.

Students require a degree of security in their relationship and need to feel that their teacher has skills, knowledge and competence. They do not like being let down by an inadequate teacher any more than they enjoy being bullied by an arrogant one.

The secret of authority is creating confidence on the part of others. To do this, you must be reasonably confident in yourself. If a teacher trusts a class and accepts the students as authorities in their own right, the students will respect authority on the part of the teacher.

It always helps if teachers:

admit their own mistakes;
laugh at anything silly they do;
ask for and accept information from the students.

Authority issues in the school

In practice, schools like every other organization function in terms of authority issues that are never full worked out. We do not normally go through life questioning all in positions of authority over us whether they be bus drivers or solicitors let alone chief executives and chairpersons of boards. In fact, most of us are remarkably docile when it comes to being told what to do. It is this that holds society together. Daily life is full of compromises and for most of us that includes the work place.

Sometimes teachers are not prepared to make the compromises at school that they make in outside life and in their own families. Many ι~ ~hers who are parents find it useful from time to time to consider how they relate to their own children at home and remind themselves of the amount of negotiation that goes on and how often their children manage to get their own way!

Students are like adults

School pupils are much like adults in most respects. For the most part they do what they are told without much questioning and are remarkably tolerant of people who instruct them. It is a real temptation for teachers to underestimate their students and to assume a lack of maturity and understanding that does them an injustice.

Certainly, all students are required to do things that ordinary adults would refuse to do or at least would be awkward about. Few adults, for instance, would put up with the typical secondary-school day of frequent subject changes or having to produce a piece of creative writing on immediate demand.

There is an inherent danger in talking down to anyone and to use youth or inexperience as a reason for so doing is to court antagonism. Students will always find subtle ways of getting their own back on a teacher who is consistently unfair with them — and it is their own interpretation of 'unfair' that influences them.

Any situation in which one group holds authority over another is potentially stressful for each group and possibly more so for the group in authority. After all it seems to be the teachers who have more nervous breakdowns not the pupils! That is why when a person is in authority they should always be exceedingly careful not to create stress by desiring an excess of influence.

A good school will always be one where there is the maximum amount of respect for everyone and the greatest amount of self-respect. There are, however, some sad creatures who enjoy authority because it allows them to wield power even at their own expense. Such teachers punish themselves as much as their pupils by keeping them in after school, giving them extra work which they have to mark, and extending the syllabus beyond what is needed for normal examination purposes.

A good question to ask yourself about how you perceive yourself as an authority figure is, 'For whose benefit do you want it — your own or your students?'

If it is for yourself, almost certainly authority issues will become causes of stress because your sense of success will depend on your self-image.

CAUSING YOUR OWN STRESS

Self-induced stress

One of the more interesting questions about teacher stress is why so much of it is self-induced. Some teachers put themselves under considerable personal stress when they do not need to. This often occurs in confrontation when a teacher will pick on a student knowing — or so one would have thought — that there will be conflict of some sort. Perhaps some teachers find it difficult just to leave well alone or they have a missionary need to improve all students.

Having too strong a sense of mission is a cause of stress. The stronger our need to achieve, the more we will be disappointed with other people's responses. Missionary spirit can soon become arrogance which other people actively resist. Sometimes the need to convert or change others arises because we are aware of our own failings but will not accept them. Low self-esteem comes about because we will not accept ourselves for what we are, and some people compensate for their own sense of failure by demanding success from others whom they believe they can influence.

Perhaps part of being a teacher is the feeling that you have the right to interfere; people must be made to learn because if they do not the teacher will be to blame. There is some truth in this but there must be something else. Schooling is organized on a timescale that does not necessarily relate to the rest of life though in the early years it relates more closely than in later ones. Teachers frequently set tasks on a time-scale that may be quite out of kilter with an individual's own timescale — the idea of the late developer illustrates this. But it means that teachers feel a compunction to make things happen on their own timescale and they consider not to do so would be a dereliction of duty. To allow children to develop in their own time would be seen as laziness on the part of the class teacher. The dilemma is that it might very well be just that — another 'no win' situation that can lead to stress since it relates closely to threats of being thought to be incompetent.

> We should not try to fulfil ourselves through other people. It is best to allow our students to learn in their own way and at their own pace. One person's sense of time is not another's.

Negotiated purposes

We can express the ideas of organizational objectives and individual needs differently by saying that if the purposes of the organization are not equally negotiated by the members, the organization will be unable to function properly and the declared objectives will not be achieved. It may be that some teachers believe that students have no right to negotiate what they do in school or even to be a party to negotiation. But negotiation is of the essence in interpersonal relationships and there can be no proper relationship between teacher and pupil if negotiation is precluded. Negotiation cannot be declined unilaterally.

Most of us will settle for a good deal less negotiation than we deserve and students are no different; but they do demand some openness to negotiation. For a teacher to refuse all negotiation even of the most trivial kind is to raise a reaction out of all proportion of its apparent cause. Head teachers are only too familiar with situations when teachers complain about a student or a whole class, and it is obvious that the teacher's own stubbornness is the cause and not any deliberate belligerence on the part of the pupil or class.

> All satisfactory personal relationships are based on negotiation in which all parties are winners and no parties are losers.

The example of school uniform

The problem of authority is epitomized in the compulsory wearing of school uniform; school uniform is a symbol. It is a surprisingly contentious topic because it seems to touch a lot of hidden sensibilities, not all of them clearly related. There are sometimes very good practical or pragmatic reasons why school students should wear a uniform, but there are no good 'objective reasons' why schoolchildren should wear uniforms. There can be more problems with school uniform than any other school matter. School uniform has become a symbol of a whole number of concerns and anxieties about schooling and is defended with considerable energy. School uniform symbolizes the success of the school in achieving everything it set out to achieve; the fact that what has been achieved may bear no relationship to the wearing of the uniform is usually irrelevant.

Uniform is held to be a visible and public sign of what the school has done. It symbolizes the success of authority − that teachers have been able to achieve what they (vaguely) promised. But the students frequently do not see it that way and do everything they can to show that they have not been controlled completely. They do all sorts of things with their uniform to show that their individuality has not been impaired and that they are still individuals. Only, perhaps, years after they have left school and are having problems of authority over others do they look back at school uniform as a symbol of stability, sound values, discipline and a respect for proper values.

This still leaves the question unanswered as to why some teachers want school uniform to be imposed for its own sake (though perhaps few give 'for its own sake' as a reason). The answer can only be that in some magical way the uniform achieves what teachers cannot achieve in their own classroom relationships.

The real symbolism of school uniform more often than not is that it gives an appearance of an achievement of values and attainment, successe and development, that have in fact not taken place nor could they under the prevailing school regime. There is no wonder that some teachers become very distressed when uniform becomes a topic of conversation.

If you feel very strongly about school uniform ask yourself why it should or should not be required of teachers. What would the consequences be if it were compulsory for teachers?

Where teachers do wear 'uniform' are the conditions the same for teachers as for students?

How do you feel about being asked to consider this?

Do you know why you feel that way?

Reinventing the school

As with many kinds of organization, if we were inventing schools today we would make them very different from the way they are. Unfortunately we have to make the best of what we have so we need to understand them particularly well. If we want to change them, however, we could begin with the things that go wrong and try to put them right rather than try a new blueprint. Since none of us is going to be able to change the whole system and we have to live with what we have, we could do worse than identify those things that cause us most concern and try to ameliorate them.

Timetabling

The day-to-day running of the school is organized through the timetable which is an attempt to allocate resources to the curriculum. The curriculum is expressed in operational terms as a series of syllabuses which indicate the content and method of what teachers and students do. The timetable is simply the allocation of people to places at specified times. It is a technical device to facilitate the management of the school and is necessary because there are so many people to be accommodated in a comparatively small space.

The timetable has no inherent magic about it; it is replicated every day wherever people gather together for a multitude of purposes, in shops, offices, railway stations, airports, bus terminals, etc. Its basic purpose is to serve the needs of the people to whom it relates and to make life materially and emotionally more comfortable for them. Timetables are comparatively simple matters to construct when the population they refer to is accurately known as in schools. Why then are school timetables such a problem for some teachers and heads?

The answer is that we start at the wrong end of the problem. Most schools take their curriculum requirements as given and then try to design a timetable round them. This sounds the most sensible and logical way to go about things but it is unrealistic. Very little of life is concerned with deciding what we want to do and then doing it. Almost everything we do in life requires us to work round circumstances as they are and to adapt to them. Then we rationalize after the event.

The reality is that there is nothing that is of itself essential to the curriculum even if a number of things would be almost universally considered desirable. Whatever is decided to be 'essential' to the curriculum will be a matter for dispute and controversy and in the end subjected to the exigencies of the timetable.

If teachers would accept practicality or pragmatism as the ground rule to their decision-making they would be saved a good deal of anguish over philosophically ideal curricula. Nowhere in real life is the desirable attainable and to expect it is to increase the frustration and consequent stress we experience.

A major cause of stress is overlooking the obvious and practical. Many concerns over the school timetable are a consequence of self-indulgence rather than reality. It really does not matter what goes into the school timetable so long as the people who have to spend time together find that time well spent.

What upsets you most about the school timetable? Who is really affected by it? Who is helped and who is hindered?

In what ways do teachers and students experience school timetables differently?

OBSESSION WITH TRIVIA

Preoccupation with detail as a stressor

Some teachers get very worked up about timetable detail. They worry if a lesson is shortened (for example, because another has overrun) or if it is cancelled (by a rehearsal or school event) or if it comes at the wrong time of day (in the afternoon instead of first thing in the morning). Some teachers want all their lessons at the beginning of the day in the (mistaken) belief that students learn better early in the morning; some want them spread throughout the week in the (mistaken) belief that students learn best when they have one session each day in a subject. Some students might learn better in any of these ways but not all, because learning patterns are very individual and to be effective must be self-determined rather than imposed.

There are several possible reasons for obsession with specific times, but the most likely reason is that such teachers are really asking for recognition which has become a desire for acknowledgement of their importance, a recognition for their work and worth. Unfortunately, some people demand recognition in terms that cannot be met because their sense of self-esteem is so low they can accept only criticism and not praise.

We need to take into account the possibility that there may be pathological considerations in many organizations which it is sometimes difficult to recognize. One way in which this shows is when teachers start niggling over small and trivial issues instead of broad concerns, especially when this takes up most of the time in formal meetings. By worrying over detail and its administrative implications teachers feel more comfortable because detail can be perceived as 'fact' and so they can draw attention to themselves through what are indisputably tangible matters.

A feeling of being unrecognized or unrewarded has nothing to do with the status of a subject taught but is a deep-seated emotional state which no amount of tinkering with in administrative terms will satisfactorily deal with. Teachers who feel their true worth is being recognized or whose real problems are receiving attention will not continue to pick away at trivial matters but will concern themselves with matters of more consequence.

If you find yourself becoming obsessed with trivial matters — which you probably see as important matters of administrative and organizational concern — you need to step outside yourself and ask, 'What would really happen if these things were left unchanged? Whose world would fall apart? Am I looking after other people's interests or my own? Am I saying no one else can find a solution without my intervention?'

Problems of holding strong views

Teachers with strong and extreme views are likely to develop a concern for detail which leads to confrontation with students and colleagues and considerable intolerance of other people's practice. We gave the example of school uniform; a concern with how students dress would be an extension of this. Another is overconcern with spelling, handwriting, neatness, timekeeping, good manners, language and so on. Ordinary daily life is filled with ambiguity and uncertainty; it is also filled with people who let us down, provide poor service, show disregard and so on. We only cope with ordinary life if we have a high level of tolerance and a sense of humour and are not too concerned about our own dignity.

If you find yourself much concerned with other people's detail, ask yourself why you are so concerned. Then ask yourself if there is any good reason why your view of detail should be better than theirs.

Attention to detail provides something of a dilemma to teachers because they want students to know how to do things properly and this tends to mean showing the one way that they consider the best way. In life outside school matters will be very different. What was exact in school becomes inexact in daily life; and what schools thought of as unimportant is of detailed significance.

HANDLING DISCIPLINE

Fear of failure

We referred earlier to the problem of authority; it will be a constant theme throughout the book because it is at the heart of many problems associated with stress. Teachers can find authority in its many forms problematical, particularly in the uncertain relationship between organizational authority and personal authority. One of the great fears that teachers have is being unable to exercise adequate authority over a class; they fear indiscipline from the students and have a horror of losing control − and, more important, fear being seen as incompetent in the process.

Young and beginning teachers particularly find discipline one of their most difficult problems. They fear being unable to control their classes and not achieving the level of class motivation of experienced teachers. They may lack confidence in themselves and fear that their intellectual inadequacies may be uncovered. They lack the skills of negotiation with a class so that an unspoken agreement can be made about what the class will accept from the teacher and what the teacher can expect from the class.

They probably have a mental picture of their own favourite teachers whom they saw as exceedingly competent and able, with a whole repertoire of tricks to keep order and make the lessons interesting, and they may be trying to model themselves on such memories. They fear loss of face, loss of confidence, professional inadequacy, running out of work for the class to do, being unable to prepare adequately and so on; all of which can be exceedingly stressful even when they are out of the classroom.

They also fear the reaction of their older colleagues − and perhaps their peers − who may find that they are not doing too well in the classroom. They may see their colleagues as the same teachers who evaluated them when they were students and have the same fear of the head that they had when at school themselves. Some of these fears are rational and realistic; without them there could be no emotional or practical preparation for the classroom and things can go badly wrong for an ill-equipped teacher. A keen teacher understandably wants to be a 'good' teacher with a natural desire to succeed − a stressful condition, self-induced but potentially creative rather than hurtful.

Beginning teachers are either too easy going with their classes or too strict. They see the most important task as being in control. This of course is right, but the question is, How do you gain control?

> The answer is naturally complex but at the core of any personal answer is the question of how the teacher negotiates agreement with the students that working together is going to be worthwhile. The students must accept that what you want them to do will be of value to them. Therefore it must also be of value to you.
>
> Some teachers ask students to do worthless tasks simply because they think this is the best way of establishing control — like copying from the board or a book, doing corrections several times.

The folk memory of schools is of quiet places where children work diligently under the stern but benevolent guardianship of respected, authoritarian but beloved teachers who kindly administer corporal punishment when it is deserved to pupils who are grateful for the discipline they are trained in. Children were naturally obedient, sat quietly without complaint, spoke respectfully to their teachers, did everything in concert and learned easily every necessary skill and moral attitude. It is unlikely that there were many schools like those in the Victorian primer, though some were closer to the myth than others.

The important aspect of this imaginary 'ideal' school is that the teachers are in charge and the students largely unquestioning; the fear of such a situation being completely overturned is strong for some teachers. There is much current discontent particularly among older teachers that students are not particularly obedient. There is so much concern that perhaps teachers need to make more concessions to personal need as students conceive it. The problem with good order is that it must be acceptable to all parties; it cannot be imposed but arises out of the circumstances, the nature of the tasks and the agreement of all those involved that certain order is the best way to achieve what is commonly agreed to be in everyone's interests, or at least in the interests of the majority.

If you insist on someone doing what they do not want to do, disobedience in some form or other will be inevitable. Many of the things we ask students to do are unreasonable even when they arise from some administrative necessity of the school's creation. It is good advice not to compel people to do what they are unwilling to do and the problem in schools is that the relationship between teacher and pupil often precludes the dialogue that is a necessary condition for compliance. A golden rule is that there can never be too much exchanging of information and feelings.

Compare what your students are required to do with what adults are required to do in everyday life. If you find yourself asking students to do what you would be unwilling to do yourself now, you should reconsider your request.

Unreasonableness

Some schools suffer from escalated unreasonableness. Schools which are out of touch with the socially determined needs of students and ignore them or, worse, deny their legitimacy are inviting the trouble they get. There have been notorious cases of schools with high indiscipline, low staff morale, much damage to property and antagonism to teachers by both students and parents. Such situations are never without cause, but once they become established they are very difficult to remedy without drastic action at the highest level.

The way to a solution, however, is clear; it is by dialogue and negotiation which will usually mean that the school has to forgo many of its impositions and relax teacher control in order to involve pupils and parents more in the management of the school. Sometimes teachers fear backtracking, seeing compromise as a climb down. Sadly the commonest organizational response, especially in the human services, is to increase control mechanisms, clamp down on deviance and rebellion, and try to impose authority simply by assertion. The effect is counter-productive and only makes things worse.

The problem for some teachers is that they do not accept pupils and parents as equal (though different) partners in the organization of the school. If they see people as inferior in some way, then the necessary compromising will be impossible and solutions to problems will be ineffective. It is, in fact, a stronger position to be able to climb down or offer compromise than to stick out for a viewpoint except, perhaps, in the most extreme of political situations. Unfortunately, some people seem to feel the need for unrelenting confrontation because they see giving in as a moral weakness whereas the truth is quite the reverse.

MAINTAINING CONTROL

Fear of chaos

Part of the fear of losing control is the fear of chaos. *Chaos* is a word much used by teachers to describe the collapse of order, control or discipline − or what they consider to be the collapse. Fear of disorder is a long-standing one in human consciousness, not least the Anglo-Saxon Protestant and Catholic consciousness. But the fear is really unfounded; human behaviour is always purposeful and in response to circumstances. Sometimes it may not be the kind of behaviour we would like but it is never purposeless, especially in the context of a formal organization such as a school.

When students behave in a disorderly fashion, they do so because they have not been dealt with in a way that is meaningful to them. When students express discontent it always relates to specific behaviour on the part of the school 'establishment'; likewise with anarchy. For one thing, anarchy requires organization and co-ordination of a particular kind. Students may be disobedient and organize protests, but they will always be less well-organised than the actions of teachers, unless the teachers have wildly miscalculated (which they occasionally do).

Fears about what students might do if they get out of hand are not fears about the students but fears within the teacher that they will not be able to cope with the response of the students; and sometimes there is a hidden guilt that the students might be right to rebel against what they are asked to do. After all, students make a major demand for fairness on the part of their teachers.

If the fear of 'anarchy' comes into your mind or colleagues start talking about it, it is worth seeking clarification as to what sort of behaviour that 'anarchy' will lead to.

Is it a fear of losing control completely, or of the students misbehaving outrageously?

Students have a very realistic view of justice and find injustice intolerable especially when it is meted out to people who have no means of redress. A lot of school 'justice' would be unacceptable outside school.

Can you think of any examples in your school where the kind of justice has been different from that current in your neighbourhood?

More often than not, chaos or anarchy is a consequence of the inability of a teacher to provide students with the activities appropriate to their needs. It means that students are not going about their work in a purposeful and self-disciplined way. It arises from a failure to be helpful enough. If a teacher cannot or will not help then the students have to help themselves which they do by trying to change the relationship with the teacher — usually by challenging their power to coerce them. Although their behaviour may appear confused and aimless, it will in fact be quite purposeful overall and an attempt to move the power in the classroom to where it can be used most helpfully.

By the large, students are pretty docile and receptive, but if they are treated to behaviour that is inappropriate they will rebel — sometimes quietly, sometimes noisily.

Think of things you are asked to do in school that you object to. In what ways are they similar to the things students are asked to do and in what ways dissimilar?

The vulnerability of performance

A teacher whose enjoyment of teaching is as a performer in the classroom — that is, who treats students as an audience — must expect audience response. The more teachers perform, the more vulnerable will they be to hostile responses when the performance is bad. For example, if teaching depends on performance what happens to that performance when the teacher feels tired, has a throat infection, is upset about some domestic matter, is worried about the cost of car repairs, etc.?

Furthermore, when teachers feel personally responsible for the performance, they are more likely to evaluate their own performance as inadequate, and be less tolerant of themselves when they do not receive the amount of 'applause' they need. So a sense of personal failure creeps into the evaluation of the lesson because it is regarded as successful not by what the students do but by how the teacher feels about his or her performance and its reception. For teachers who are lecturers in colleges the dilemma is even greater for unless they can deliver their prepared act to an approving response, they can only feel that they have failed.

Most teachers need the warm approval of their students to obtain the satisfactions they require from the job. Many teachers are really actors in a different setting. Without success in the classroom, there is no point in being a teacher. But since students can tire of performance especially when it makes unwelcome demands on them the counteraction they can take is limited. They cannot walk out at the interval or refuse to come to the next performance.

Shared authority in learning

The authority of the teacher in the role of teacher is, of course, separate from the authority that lies within the discipline of the subject that is taught. Nowadays teachers no longer seem to say 'You must believe this because I tell you so even if your experience tells you the opposite'. Authority does not lie in the person who teaches but in the knowledge the learner has about how they are learning.

Learners learn best when they have insight into how they are learning and they can then enter a mutual learning relationship. They have a right to say: 'I am tired; I need a break' or 'Can you go over that again I really don't think I understand it?' or 'Can we have another look at so and so; I really think we could do something different with it?' Most teachers would claim to be delighted if a student were to say that, but the truth is that many would not because they would see assurance on the part of the learner even as learner as a threat to their authority. There is some evidence that this perceived threat is greater the older the students get.

Yet effective teaching must surely lead to learners becoming increasingly competent in what they are learning. The more students understand what they are learning the more responsible they become for how they learn and better informed about what they are going to learn; that is, they will be better able to make judgements about the next step in their learning, and this may not always be in the direction the teacher had intended to go. The job of the teacher is to help the learners with their learning not to make the learners do just what the teacher wants. A great deal of teaching takes the responsibility away from the student in order to maintain the authority of the teacher.

Good teaching and good classroom management should be directed towards increasing the autonomy of the students, their independence of the teacher and an increased sense of responsibility for their own learning. The problem for many teachers is that they are more dependent on their students than their students are on them. The only way some teachers can feel rewarded is if the dependence of their students is continually acknowledged.

Look carefully from time to time at how much you are doing unnecessarily for other people and for your students. We all find it difficult to let go of the reins and we can waste valuable emotional energy supervising students excessively.

For some teachers, excessive energy spent on continually monitoring student work contributes to stress-related sickness.

Student success

It is a strange quirk of our educational system that the actual development of students is really towards not increased autonomy but increased dependence. In the nursery school, teachers can work with children cooperatively only because children will respond if their interest and attention have been captured. Teachers of young children aim to increase the independence of their pupils by encouraging them to take more and more independence for themselves. Success is marked by children making a sequence of decisions for themselves to their own benefit.

But gradually as students rise through the system, this independence is curtailed and reaches its climax in the university examination system which not only requires a very high level of conformity but stamps a tight classification on its evaluation. Perhaps the reality is that educational systems work for those who choose to be socialized into them and not for those who do not. Since teachers are, by virtue of their training, successful products of the system they may not understand the position of the much larger number of people who also went to school and decided that a career back in school was not for them. Perhaps teachers should not worry too much that what they try to do is rejected by so many; after all the rejection does not really hurt all that much unless you let it.

Some teachers are worried by what they see as an increasingly restrictive system. They feel themselves caught up in the same conformist system as their students and want to break out.

This feeling can be overcome by becoming involved in a course or curriculum project where you can determine what is required of students. Or go for promotion to as senior a position as you need.

3
STAFF-STUDENT RELATIONSHIPS

● Choices that can cause stress ● Pushing yourself too far ● Personality characteristics and stress ● Personal standards can cause stress ● Coping with a sense of failure ● Sense of time and priority

CHOICES THAT CAN CAUSE STRESS

Since stress is something that affects a person as an individual, the only way we can deal with stress is in a personal way. In the end all coping with stress comes down to the individual and will always involve a measure of self-help. Therefore, an essential element in coping with stress is personal insight.

The remarkable thing about stress is that most individuals find it exceedingly difficult to deal with on their own; in some way or another they always involve others in the situation. Often we expect the causes to go away of their own accord or for someone to take pity on us and take them away. For example, a teacher who is snowed under with marking books and finds a log-jam each weekend building up over the term may find it easier to blame someone else for the predicament. Instead of realizing that the pile is of their own making, they may blame the head for requiring so much marking to be done, or 'the system' for being so demanding, or 'the pupils' for not doing their work properly, or whatever. The solution like the cause lies with the teacher who could have found a more convenient way of dealing with the work load; the fact that many sensible solutions are unacceptable is one of the reasons the work-load has become unbearable. Teachers who find ways around being overworked do not suffer from stress.

> When you find that you are overworking, ask 'Who insists that I do this? What are the consequences for me if I don't do it?'

Most stress problems have quite easy common sense solutions but for some people the problem is that the solution is so easy; they want solutions that are as difficult as the problem or they feel cheated. To deal with stress within ourselves we must have a clear insight into what makes us tick and what gets us down.

Choosing to teach

A good starting point for understanding yourself as a teacher is to try to find out why you wanted to be a teacher in the first place.

> What was the attraction of the job? Why did you seek to be a member of this particular profession and not one of the other helping professions?

After all, you did choose to be a teacher and exercised that choice in preference to many others. No one can say they had no choice at all over a job even in periods of high unemployment. Even those who 'drifted' into teaching were exercising a proper choice, even if they were not fulfilling a lifelong ambition.

There seem to be two important aspects of the choice to be a teacher. One has to do with the age of the students they like working with — five-year-olds or adults, for instance. The other is a sense of personal fulfil-ment — the kinds of skills and interests they want to work with and that they enjoy; things like enjoying mathematics or working with instruments.

These two dimensions are about people and about subjects and the balance between them is unique to each of us. Some veer to preferring people and will therefore not mind too much what they teach, while for others the subject will be the more important factor and they will always want to teach it in the optimum circumstances.

> Try to decide which matters most to you: the teaching of the subject or working with young people. If you come under stress it will most likely be in the area that matters most to you personally. This is because you get more satisfaction from these. Job dissatisfaction is the best predictor of stress.

Associated with this choice of teaching as a profession is whether we see the job as being for the benefit of the client (i.e. the student) or our own. There is nothing wrong in either but the cause of stress will be different. A client-centred approach will lead to stress in terms of demands from students which cannot be fully met while a self-orientated approach will lead to stress related to a sense of justification, reward, self-fulfilment and good opinion of peers and superiors.

A key question for yourself in considering what you want out of teaching is whether you look for promotion or wish to stay in the classroom.

It is important for each of us to have as clear and realistic a picture of ourself as possible in terms of personal strengths and weaknesses. However, we are not always good judges of our strengths and weaknesses. We need help in determining them and may also fail to see that what we consider to be strengths others consider weaknesses and what we think of as weaknesses have great potential as strengths. Most weakness can be turned to advantage when properly understood, and we need to assess our supposed weaknesses if we are to achieve the sense of personal esteem we all require to function fully in our social lives.

Because schools are usually highly evaluative and competitive institutions, teachers tend to be over-critical of one another and often unfairly evaluative of themselves. They also have to compete for acknowledgement, etc. If children are required to be high achievers by the school the teachers will find themselves required to be high achievers too, even if the measurement is made through the students. A problem is that some classes will have students in them who are 'cleverer' than their teachers and nearly all classes will have students who are higher achievers in some way or another than their teachers. For example, most teachers over thirty find themselves much less able in matters of computers than their students.

It is part of the nature of teaching that some students will be more able than their teachers and others will rate their teachers as of little consequence. The problem is that sometimes these quite different responses can upset teachers a good deal. Teachers who sees themselves in competition with their students – and some do – will be under some stress while those who see themselves as helpers and facilitators may feel no stress at all.

> Competing with students can be a cause of stress because teachers can never really win. Students will always have the advantage that they are students, no matter how novel the area of rivalry may be.

PUSHING YOURSELF TOO FAR

Performance

We mention in Chapter 2 the vulnerability of some teachers who are much interested in themselves as 'performers' or 'actors' and make the classroom a little theatre. Undoubtedly some aspects of teaching require acting skills; simply facing a group of students is a public performance. When people speak of teachers as 'characters' they are probably referring to some quality of acting − though whether it was well-intended or merely eccentricity would need to be determined − and there is a sort of folk belief that teachers should be good actors. But really, acting has very little to do with teaching though it may have a good deal to do with entertainment and that may or may not be a help to learning.

The problem of teaching as entertainment is that it requires a singular audience reaction on the part of the class as a whole. If it is successful the teacher benefits but if it is unsuccessful everyone loses. If the class will not respond to the performance the teacher must have recourse to sanctions because the audience is captive and cannot go away or be replaced by the next house. When theatrical performance succeeds it can be resoundingly good but when it fails the teacher loses such face that they may never recover. Teachers who go for 'performance' will always put themselves at risk and discipline will suffer. The organizing of seven or eight successful performances a day is a tall order in view of changing moods, enthusiasm and energy. In any case, conventional wisdom says that students come to school to learn not to be entertained.

> If you enjoy acting in front of a class of students, would you not enjoy the satisfactions of an adult or mixed audience more? Can you find openings for your thespian skills elsewhere?

Domination

It may be that some teachers get their 'kicks' out of being in command, of dominating the class from the front. This seems remarkably like self-indulgence however well it may be done. To keep the attention of an audience and to deal with the awkward member, the actor has to manipulate. Some teachers manage to do this but there are dangers in the need to manipulate and control; for one thing, an enemy or butt has to be found within the audience itself and that may mean some psychological abuse.

Those who want to dominate a group of people place themselves under considerable stress because no one can be in charge for so long just by themselves. Being continually in command can be enervating because the need to control replaces the need to provide worthwhile activity. Charging up and down the rows cajoling recalcitrant pupils may look all right in a comedy film but it has nothing to do with teaching or class management. Just feeling the need to be in front all the time can be exhausting; the secret is to help the students to do any 'performing' that is necessary and to keep teacher energies for when they can be usefully and purposefully called on.

PERSONALITY CHARACTERISTICS AND STRESS

Coping types

It is worth recalling that all jobs require some form of coping for them to be done; no job does itself and we all find different ways of doing them and dealing with the difficulties that arise. But no job should be designed to get the better of its doer so we need to take care that we do not let it get on top of us, or be too great a challenge.

One of the difficulties of working with other people is that we take the lead from them rather than determining for ourselves what the job is that we are going to do. We sometimes become unnecessarily competitive and try to do the job better than others, but in their way, so putting an impossible constraint on ourselves. In this way we put ourselves at risk emotionally as well as physically.

Writers on occupational stress identify two types of person: one is liable to suffer stress unduly and with harmful physical effects while the other is able to avoid the harmful effects. They have somewhat unimaginatively been termed *Type A* and *Type B* behaviours and are characterized as follows.

Type A

A Type-A person generally has most of the following characteristics:

has high ambition;
is hyperactive, 'driven';
is authoritarian or autocratic;
is a perfectionist;
is over-conscientious;
is exceedingly energetic;
tends to be frenetic and in a rush;
is highly volatile and difficult to pin down;
dominates other people;
has a great sense of urgency;
is a workaholic.

Type B

A Type-B person, on the other hand, is usually recognizable by these characteristics:

is phlegmatic and 'laid back';
is not highly ambitious;
is relaxed and easy-going;
tends to be *laissez-faire*;
may even be serene;
sometimes, at least, carefree;
is not easily troubled;
does not live for their work.

You should be able to recognize yourself as one or other of these types − the 'driven' Type A or the 'laid-back' Type B. If you find yourself Type A, what do you intend to do about it?

Many Type-A people decide to do nothing about it and even consider the advice to do something to be an impertinence.

The causes of stress relate not only to professional standards but to the individual perception of professional standards. It is a matter of personal interpretation or appraisal that leads to the stressor being real or otherwise. For some, teaching is a relaxing, easy-going profession and some schools are relaxed, easy-going places to be in. One teacher may find sixth-form work comfortable and stimulating while another may find it too demanding and worrying. One teacher might enjoy working with difficult children because of the constant variety and high energy levels of the students while another finds the whole idea of 'difficult' students makes them count the days to premature early retirement.

Personal satisfactions

In coping with the process of teaching we need to know what we want out of the experience and what we feel is necessary to achieve it. Wants and needs are, of course, not the same but it is no use looking for satisfactions that the job cannot provide either intrinsically or by attribution. In the end job satisfaction is concerned with the gratification of needs not wants. We may want approval for what we do from someone in authority above us but if we only receive it from our students it may not be enough.

> See if you can think of three kinds of approval you want from your boss. (You need to decide who your boss is!) What happens when you do not get it?
>
> Now try to think of three kinds of approval you want from your students. What happens when you do not get it?
>
> Do you think these wants are the same as needs?

One of the difficulties of teaching is that while teachers get older the students stay the same age. One might expect the satisfactions from teaching for a 25-year-old to be different from those of a 45-year-old and this may be one reason why promotion becomes more important as we get older. Promotion involves more relationships with our contemporaries, whereas a young teacher may be virtually contemporary with his or her students, especially in sixth forms or further education colleges – but not, of course, in primary schools where parental feelings are likely to be strong.

While the student body remains comparatively immature, the gap emotionally between teacher and student widens. Even teachers of infants may feel further apart from them as their own children grow up. Often teachers of young children make a particular effort to enjoy 'adult' interests in their social life for this reason. It is perhaps more difficult for teachers of teenage students to recognize the age and cultural gap since many adults enjoy the same kind of things as adolescents though in different ways. But those differences may be difficult to accept.

Bluffing

There is a great deal of bluff in being a teacher, especially when dealing with adolescents. The wish to bluff arises partly from our own school experiences when we have seen it succeed and partly because there is always an element of uncertainty in group situations; people might not react as expected. But there is a danger in taking it too far because this leads to confusion all round.

There is always a temptation to treat a class as if it were all of one mind; yet classes are not nearly so homogeneous as some teachers like to imagine. This lack of homogeneity becomes important when sanctions are contemplated against a whole class or there is some injustice in teacher behaviour. Sometimes a teacher will threaten a whole class with punishment; sometimes a whole school or college is punished. At this point the unity of the class, etc., is tested and usually found wanting.

Some teachers have a problem of both wishing to have a close relationship with their students and also being able to punish wrongdoers. Such punishment often becomes scapegoating because each student punished is symbolic rather than personally deserving. If punishment is a consequence of bluff being called, then the teacher loses face from which it will be difficult to recover. There must be a question around why a teacher should want both to bluff and to punish. The behaviour that is punished is a consequence of the teacher's own relationships with the class.

If you find yourself resorting to punishment a great deal – as in punishing the same few students or threatening a whole class – you need to reflect on your own style of teaching. It is unlikely that the class is at fault, rather that you are being unreasonable towards them.

Talk the situation through with a trusted colleague or senior colleague and seek new ways of doing things. By asking for help you will receive more respect from your colleagues than you would by blundering on alone.

Along with scapegoating and the blaming of others for our own behaviour is the problem of projecting onto others the problems we ourselves have. Teachers sometimes misunderstand student behaviour and ascribe reasons that are creations of their own imagination. We all project anxieties and motives onto others, especially when they are a collective 'audience', but we can easily misjudge reactions by interpreting them as if they were our own.

Few teachers were blameless students themselves and even if they did not actually badly misbehave will have dreamed of it. It is tempting therefore to ascribe to our students the same emotional activity that was ours; second-guessing of any kind brings problems even when it is correct! More often than not students will react in quite unsophisticated ways; if they are inattentive they are simply bored rather than plotting some great rebellion. When bored they are inattentive!

Boredom is the greatest cause of inattention and indiscipline.

Teachers must accept responsibility for their own behaviour and its consequences and not look for dark plots among their charges. Students are very much in the hands of their teachers and are much exposed by what teachers do to them. Even asking a question which a student cannot answer may be much more cruel than it appears. Teachers are often quite unaware how they expose their students' weaknesses and should not be surprised if they occasionally hit back.

Think of the things you most hated your teachers doing to you. Most of them you will try to avoid but there may be some you find yourself prone to. Can you identify them?

If you find that you are deliberately doing things to students because you remember that they are disliked, you are probably suffering some stress from that class. That is why you are trying to hurt them.

PERSONAL STANDARDS CAN CAUSE STRESS

Setting an example

Many teachers feel that they must be exemplary in their behaviour and that they must set a good example to students. 'Setting an example' is, however, a vague concept liable to reinterpretation according to circumstance and often an excuse for punishment or sanctions. There is, of course, everything to be commended in teachers who manage to exemplify in their own lives the precepts that they lay before others, though it becomes something of an effort in practice and there are difficulties when one falls short. But it becomes a larger problem when the precepts of the teacher become requirements for the students who have not been a party to an agreement about what they should or should not do.

If you believe you ought to set an example, do you know for whose benefit you are really doing it? Do you get a feeling of self-righteousness by doing so? Or do you enjoy the discomfort the effort produces?

What does a self-awareness that you are setting a good example do to you?

Moral standards and partnership

Learning requires a partnership in setting standards and that means more than just agreeing to what you are told. Schools tend to set moral standards as if they existed quite apart from the people to whom they refer and without realizing that codes of behaviour only work when they are acceptable to those to whom they apply. Teachers sometimes have to learn that their own exemplary behaviour might not be copied by their students but that their students are nevertheless not less moral as a consequence.

We have mentioned how some teachers impose on themselves standards that are beyond their capability to sustain. It is a measure of good social adjustment not to overstretch yourself but there are a lot of social conventions that encourage us to overachieve. It should be remembered that there is no recognition for overachievement as such, rather the reverse.

In fact if what one requires is attention or recognition in the ordinary way of things then underachievement may be a better objective; or, by being deviant and not conforming to the current norms. This is what children do who are 'attention seekers' and some teachers are just the same but a bit older! The need to overachieve arises from a personal uncertainty and insecurity and it is better to look to the causes of that rather than to push yourself beyond the limits of coping.

You should be able to recognize what overachievers are because you will have had them as students. Do you recognize yourself in them? What do you do to help them? How can you apply these ideas to yourself?

Teachers may have doubts about their own careers when they hear of students being very successful in other walks of life — and also being high earners — but everyone experiences that sometime in life. Parents may share all these feelings about their children as well; teachers are not the only victims of their aspirations.

When we are feeling a bit down in our job, hearing of another person's success can increase our sense of depression. We can lift the depression by looking at the parts of our job that we have not fully exploited and use the momentary disappointment as a spur to further achievement.

Criteria of success

As with any other career, teaching has its success streams, its career routes and its failure tracks. It is not too difficult to have high morale in the early years of a job, but it can become increasingly difficult as life goes on particularly if our contemporaries become highly successful and achieve good promotion.

COPING WITH A SENSE OF A FAILURE

Of course, some people do not set up for themselves a clear career path and so do not enter the 'rat race'. Others, particularly women, may have dual careers — family and profession — and this may become increasingly true for some men. But for every one of us, however 'successful' we may be, there are life crises which occur irrespective of the track we are on because we are essentially person-based.

Very successful people may feel failures from time to time and wonder whether they have chosen the right profession. There may even be a correlation between the need to achieve (whether fulfilled or not) and emotional crises. Public figures are notorious for their personal problems because they place themselves under the stress of needing approval from so many quarters. Mid-life crises and mid-career crises often coincide for the reason that they are often related.

It is worthwhile trying to separate what you do in your private life from what you do in your career. It is better to attempt a supportive parallelism between the two so that success in one (e.g. your private life) does not depend on your career. Success in your public life can be balanced by the quality of private life.

Fortunately, we all grow wiser, maturer, and more self-confident as the years go by and we develop a sense of values that increasingly serves our needs rather than challenges us. At 45 we no longer value what was important for us at 25. Usually — though not always — we mellow and it is the process of becoming easier about things round about us that gives us comfort.

As we grow older we become aware of our colleagues who may have achieved more materially but who are in a state of personal crisis because they have found more and more to cope with, more and more burdens passed on to them by others. When we notice this in other people we can usefully take stock and look at our own achievement in terms of the quality of life.

It is worth recalling that real power in any job lies with those at the bottom. They have nothing to lose from doing things their own way. They are beholden to no one. They can more easily cause disruption than those at the top and they are virtually beyond harm because their bosses cannot afford to lose face by blaming them unfairly. In a great many ways, being at the bottom is best because even if there is the ultimate sanction (dismissal — which is rare in teaching) the move to another bottom position is much easier than it is from one superior position to another.

In teaching it is still the work of the class teacher that is most highly spoken of and which, in spite of all the talk, is most coveted.

School rules

Most schools have rules, some of which will be explicit and rather more will be implicit. One stressful aspect of these is that all staff may not approve of them — regulations about uniform being a common area of disagreement. Furthermore, even when staff accept them they do not enforce them equally or are invidious with regard to penalties for breaking them.

The difficulty with all rules is that they are intended to simplify affairs but in practice often complicate matters. The reason is that they may force a polarization of response which means that conflict is more likely. Each rule becomes the source of likely dispute so the more rules the more disputes by and large. Even when the conflict is latent, it will place some

people in a stressful situation because they are apprehensive about what
will happen if they are forced to challenge them.

For some people, the prospect of breaking rules or going against
'authority' is a considerably distressing prospect. Other teachers may
decide to overlook the intellectual or moral problems of school rules in
the interests of earning themselves a good opinion and so secure promotion or good references.

SENSE OF TIME AND PRIORITY

Pacing

It is not always easy, of course, to decide what is personally and/or
professionally important, but it may be easier to decide on what is urgent
and therefore needs to be attended to more quickly. This is where
prioritizing and pacing become linked. If we all paced our work properly
and used good time-management presumably we would all complete the
work with fewer hassles. Fortunately, human beings do not behave like
automata so we are never free from moods, preferences, idiosyncrasies,
fluctuations in enthusiasm, preoccupations, and so on, all of which make
straightforward 'rational' behaviour impossible.

Journalists notoriously work best to deadlines and so do many other
people, doing a job only when its completion is just about due. (Some
people always manage just to miss a deadline, having discovered that in
any case they are just as well off!) Frequently we switch tasks from one
priority to another as we manipulate our work-load. At other times we
have high energy and cram a lot into a short time while at others
everything seems to be spaced out over quite a long, leisured period. Few
of us keep up the same pace all the time; indeed to do so is to put
ourselves under extreme pressure and to become stressed.

We have to decide for ourselves which ways work best for us — there is
no one best way — and this will usually mean bringing variety into our
work schedules. When we have work that is tedious, it is often better to
parcel it out and do a little at a time but some people like to get rid of it
all at once.

Perhaps those teachers who like to undertake external examining prefer,
for the most part, to complete all their tedious work as quickly as possible
since examination papers have to be marked in a very brief time. But
teachers who dislike tedium will allot themselves papers to mark in
batches spread over a set period of time — and then try to add an extra

one or two to each bunch to get the job over more quickly. How you arrange your work will depend on your comfort level and whether you like your adrenalin to flow in the excitement of last-minute rushing.

To pace our work we have to have a clear idea of what the work is. Of course, this is not always possible if we have not done the job before, which is often the case. We then have to rely on our experience and try to identify what the work is like. Is organizing a school fair the same as producing a school play? Is producing a school magazine the same as producing a school brochure? Is teaching 5A the same as teaching the Lower Sixth? Is being a governor the same as being a member of a parish council?

Whatever the means by which we identify the nature of the job, we have to organize it and control it. Often a task is embedded in a network of associated tasks of which we are not always aware at the beginning. We have all been persuaded to undertake some representative role such as school delegate to a local teachers' group. 'It's only two hours twice a year', we are told only to discover that is more likely three hours once a month on the same day as our favourite television series.

Then there are the unexpected but urgent demands the administration makes of us, always unexpectedly and with a timescale that cuts across our own. For some reason these external demands always have to be given a higher priority than our usual work and it is often very difficult to decide how far we can reorder the priorities decided by someone else, especially when they are in authority over us.

There are many ways of pacing ourselves but they require a conscious effort in good time. If this doesn't come to us naturally we have to work at it by reflecting on our bad feelings when we have failed to plan ahead and by creating a readiness in our minds that will set us up for preparation when the next occasion likely to cause discomfort arises.

> We learn by reflecting on our mistakes until we bring forward the response time sufficiently. In this way whether or not we are naturally methodical, we can begin to plan our time and work-load very carefully.

For example, we can start listing our tasks for the day and placing them in priority, even allocating times when we want to do them. In this way we become aware of our natural rhythms and pacing and having disciplined ourselves to a methodical pattern, we begin to follow it on future occasions because it is more comfortable for us. However, if we prefer a level of discomfort in everything we do, we can still permit that discomfort but in such a way that we still complete our tasks in the time we allocate ourselves but without undue stress. Some people write lists, allocate times and priorities, then throw the list away and forget it. They still seem to survive happily.

In a job such as teaching, neat and tidy prioritizing and organizing of work-loads is difficult. We may organize our work with students reasonably well, but our own work is not so easily dealt with. There will always be pressing demands from others, especially colleagues who require help from us with some urgency and often messiness.

4
DEVIANCE AND NORMALITY
IN SCHOOL

● Coping with power struggles ● Why teachers become alienated
● Dealing with contrary students ● Finding benefits in school
● Why schools cause problems ● Coping with freedom ● Success
and failure of students ● Understanding student reactions ● Problems of caring for students

COPING WITH POWER STRUGGLES

School organization is intended to bring order, control, predictability and
security to people who have to work together towards mutually acceptable
goals. The problem is that mutually acceptable goals are never actually
negotiated. While teachers may agree with what the school is set up to do
they have joined voluntarily but the students have probably had no
choice. Yet all the members of the school are expected to work together
harmoniously even though the potential for conflict of interest is studiously
overlooked in most schools. This has the consequence that an important
aspect of organizational behaviour that relates to the exercise of power
and the nature of authority and its legitimacy will be discounted.

The ways in which power is exercised and/or resisted is 'political'
behaviour and is characteristic of all organizations, hence of all schools.
That is not to say that every person − teacher and pupil − is actively
engaged in the overt pursuit of power, but it does mean that no redistri-
bution of power or influence can take place outside its political implications.

The normal distribution of resources of any kind is political behaviour
since it establishes the status of members in the school organization.

Because schools habitually ignore the existence of political behaviour, in the preceding sense, many teachers are unaware that many of their discontents arise for political reasons. The starting point for dealing with such pressures is to recognize political activity as natural and normal and to become as involved as you feel comfortable.

Different interests

One of the problems for schools is that there are effectively two separated classes of membership (and possibly more if we include ancillary staff of one sort and another) who are always considered separately for management purposes. These are the teachers and the students. This functional or pragmatic distinction raises important organizational and management issues.

For one thing, it is generally assumed that the interests of the two groups are not identical; also that the interests of teachers have priority. When choices have to be made they are usually in favour of the teachers and maintain their interests. The reason is that teachers hold most of the power in the school and normally students do not take part in decision-making. There are very good reasons why this should be and most teachers would claim that they make decisions in such a way that student interests are safeguarded.

But the problem is that a group of members which feels that it is excluded from the decision-making process (however the situation be defined) will feel itself disadvantaged and will behave in an alienated way as a consequence. There will, therefore, be a diversion of energy away from co-operative activity towards maintaining the separation and perhaps pointing up the consequences by disruptive behaviour; this will happen on both sides.

Teachers often dislike the behaviour of people in industry and like to think schools are different. In superficial ways they are different but in essential ways they are not. A starting point for coping with 'industrial' relations in school is to recognize them for what they are – power struggles between individuals and groups.

Organizational restrictions

By its very nature, organization reduces the amount of freedom available to everyone in the school. That is not to deny that more things are possible through collective activity than by individuals alone but once individuals are organized they become circumscribed by the organization in some way whatever position they hold.

Some people are prepared for this and see it as a trade-off against the disadvantages of being on their own; they see organization as being supportive, facilitative and generally helpful. But other people see organization as restrictive, reactive and confining and struggle to be free of their constraints.

WHY TEACHERS BECOME ALIENATED

Most people compromise — at least most of the time — but some fall into an extreme position being either overly dedicated to a particular form of school organization or actively rebellious against the norms and values of their school. By and large neither extreme position is helpful in bringing about necessary changes, but they do test out the nature and extent of organizational freedom that is possible.

Many teachers who have become disenchanted with the school take up active positions in opposition. Often they join teachers unions and then find a conflict of interest between loyalty to the school and the head, and loyalty to the union. For some teachers this tension can be unbearable. The only solution is to choose one loyalty or the other.

Most teachers belong to schools where there is the wish to create the greatest freedom for the greatest number compatible with what the head believes to be the best interests of the members — teachers and students. To make a school responsive to its members there must be a continual process of negotiation and renegotiation of the meaning of membership for each individual. This means that people will change their roles and positions and the structures will change.

Indeed, structures have to change continually as the organization of the school develops because the original structure of relationships changes over time. To achieve this everyone must have the same standing in the negotiation process; all must be open to the changes necessary for them. This creates difficulties within the power structure as some people may be unwilling to change because they foresee a loss of status. For many teachers this is a problem because they perceive any change as an undermining of their authority; for example, the substituting of 'student power' or 'parent power' for the power they themselves previously had.

Anyone who feels that their control over their circumstances has been arbitrarily taken away will experience emotional difficulties and stress. Many teachers find it difficult to accept that in purely organizational terms they have rights no different from their students.

The only way to begin coping with a situation that we view differently from others is to reframe our view of the situation. We do this by a sequence of restating and in different words how we perceive the situation until an alternative way of thinking about it becomes clear

---

Attitudes to one another

Effective membership of any organization requires us to change our attitudes to what is going on in a constant monitoring process. People who are not open to changing their attitudes are prone to collisions with others who are engaged in the process of adaptation and change, as well as others who have adopted equally intransigent positions.

DEALING WITH CONTRARY STUDENTS

Attitudes of students to teachers do actually change and there is nothing positive to be gained from not accepting such changes. If a teacher is used to the unquestioning acceptance of orders, and encounters a student who questions them there is nothing to be gained from simply standing on the dignity of position. We must try to understand why student attitudes have changed.

Students have a right to be treated as 'equals' in response to their questions whether or not this indicates a changing relationship between students and teachers. If the questioning is the consequence of a general trend, resistance is no means of dealing with it since it will lead simply to stress.

> When there seems to be a conflict between people that relates to status, it is useful to imagine the roles reversed. This enables a more appropriate evaluation to be made of what is happening.

Equality of status does not mean equality of power in the school but rather that individuals are given equal consideration in matters that concern them. Teachers and students should have equal status as 'citizens' of the school even though they have quite different roles and positions. Without this levelling in relationships, the making of mutual agreements is not possible because there can be no equality of commitment on each side.

Many schools try to make the relationship unequal in the interests of the power structure but the effect is ultimately disruptive and leads to withdrawal of commitment and even rebellion. The danger in schools is that teachers make the 'immaturity' of their students the excuse for giving them lower status in decision-making, even where the outcomes concern them as much as the teacher. Unfortunately immaturity is a very slippery concept and has little to do with age, however plausible it may seem in the context of the normal school.

Nor is the plea of greater experience on the part of the teacher an answer against a student's point of view since there are difficulties in defining the quality and relevance of experience. It is always dangerous to claim to know better than anyone else as an excuse for not explaining matters.

> The best response is always to take question etc. at its face value and with the same seriousness the questioner gives it so that both sides level in the interchange.

If a matter cannot be resolved by mature discussion then there is an important issue about the nature of relationships. We cannot unilaterally decide the status of anyone, least of all ourselves, without being measured against the realities of the organization.

Member benefits

Schools exist for the benefit of their members; members do not exist for the benefit of the school. This not to say that these benefits will be delivered equally and fairly but no one would willingly stay in an organization did they not believe it was in their interests to do so. Presumably when teachers or students cease to perceive any benefit they will want to leave and if they are prevented from leaving they will rebel.

Unfortunately, what I believe to be in your interests may not be believed by you so the matter becomes somewhat complicated. What an individual requires of a school may have little or nothing to do with the declared purposes and objectives of the school — if anyone has bothered to try to state what they are. Just because a school sets itself the objective of assisting students to achieve high grade A levels, it does not follow that all the students will accept this as a legitimate goal for themselves.

FINDING BENEFITS IN SCHOOL

Everyone should feel that there is some benefit in being a member of the school. When a member feels there is nothing, there will be trouble. But there is a difficulty in that very few people know in advance what they want out of being in a school and then they usually make their evaluation retrospectively.

It can be a cause of considerable stress to find that a school you joined hoping for a great sense of satisfaction has turned out to be one that offers little but frustration and a strong sense of dissatisfaction.

You may be able to change matters if you take up the situation with the head. On the whole, heads want their colleagues to feel fulfilled rather than disappointed.

We often cause ourselves needless stress by not sharing our responses with the very people we believe are responsible for them

---

Importance of processes

One of the problems that schools have is that objectives often seem to be more important than processes. That is, when teachers are questioned about what goes on in the school they will generally talk of objectives, of what they hope to achieve. Much less readily will they talk about the processes by which they hope to achieve these objectives. Unless schools are clear about how they want to do things there is little point in them deciding what they want to do, though this may appear to go against the conventional wisdom which declares that until you know what you want to do you cannot decide how to do it.

Schools like a number of other institutions such as hospitals are founded on a certain view of relationships and values about people which determine not only what they do but how they do it. The order of thinking is important because unless we understand it correctly we shall never know how people fit into the system. Organizational response to individuals who suffer stress is a consequence of the dominant view about the processes people engage in not about objectives.

One problem of objectives for organizations that are intended to serve the needs of their members is that you cannot decide what the members want before they join. And once they join there is a necessary process of dialogue (negotiation) if they are to feel joining to be a worthwhile activity. The fact that schools are rigidly bound by convention and their statutory requirements (i.e. their being established by law) does not change the nature of essential organizational dynamics.

The effect of much school organization is to cut off a number of students who do not fit into the neat categories administrators like and this sets up some kind of hostile interaction with other members of the school. Yet this alienation of marginal members − that is, members who are made to be marginal − can only be to the loss of the organization as a whole because it is always the marginal members who are the source of information about where the organization ought to be going. The reason is that they are the ones whose sights are outward into the wider environment while the conventional and 'central' members see nothing to question within the organization. The students who cause the most trouble are the source of 'data' about what organizational (e.g. curricular) changes will be necessary in the school before long.

> What is true of students as marginal members can also be true of teachers.

WHY SCHOOLS CAUSE PROBLEMS

In a number of important ways schools cause the very problems they are often meant to prevent. For example, they are supposed to be supportive and protective and to enable many things to be done that could not be done otherwise. To an extent these qualities will always be present for some members but it is unlikely that they will be true for all members − teachers as well as students − even in the most benign environments.

Very few schools can generate all the resources they need at a given time and when they do generate them they tend to be unevenly distributed among the members. The reason is that some members are considered (or consider themselves) to be more important than others and have the power to reinforce their position. Whenever a school cuts back on resources it does so with what are considered the less important activities though in reality they might not be so.

In schools 'minority' subjects are always cut back first even though they may be the areas of new and strategic development. Schools also introduce new developments at the margins to try them out before adoption at the centre, but they are always vulnerable until they have been supported by the security of centrality where most power lies.

Organizational restriction

School organization always restricts members in some ways even though it might be helpful to others by routinizing behaviour in such a way that initiative and freedom are channelled. Many teachers welcome this process because it enables them to work more efficiently and waste less time. Yet often teachers have been recruited because they are 'high fliers' or independently minded individuals so they find the organization restrictive because it denies them the very kind of freedom they flourish in. It is almost impossible to recruit people who will at one and the same time support the status quo and be imaginative and creative.

There are many problems around creativity in school organization that are virtually unresolvable when they have to function in a tight administrative or bureaucratic culture. While most teachers settle for a quiet life most of the time they nevertheless try to keep themselves independent of organizational pressures because they do not want to be overwhelmed by them. This means that heads may see them as uncommitted or unenthusiastic or even lacking in drive and ambition; but for the teachers it is a way of retaining their integrity.

Teachers who become highly committed to a particular form of school organization often get hurt because others do not share their enthusiasm and do not provide the wholehearted support that is demanded.

For many people, keeping their head down is the best way to survive.

Small schools tend to be more restrictive than larger ones do, though in some circumstances the reverse may be the case according to the kind of leadership exercised by the head. In a small organization the number of people with whom we relate is smaller and it may be more difficult to find someone we naturally warm to, while in a large organization not only may there be more choice but we can hide more easily from those we do not like.

On the other hand in small schools a close mutual relationship might be rewarding while in a large school it might be difficult for us to make contact with the people we most wish to work with. By and large, larger organizations will be better resourced, have greater variety and flexibility in their procedures, have more 'slack' in the system that can cope with variety of behaviour and there will be more people to share ideas and interests. Of course, some people just prefer the intimacy of small schools while others prefer the anonymity of large ones.

> The secret of survival in any organization is to make sure 'the organization' or whoever represents it to you does not take you over.

COPING WITH FREEDOM

Freedom defined

An important concept in the theory of organizations is that of freedom. As we have seen, freedom is not a consequence of any form of organization itself since organization is an attempt to restrain and control. But sometimes we are able to do things we could not otherwise do simply because the situation has been brought under systematic control. It is impossible to play any sport or game without organization and many people find freedom in the form of better health as a consequence of playing sports.

By and large freedom is not a function of organization itself and we should not look for it to be so. Freedom is a function of the way we think about ourselves and the situations we find ourselves in. For example, a music teacher is not free to teach any subject he or she likes but can make wide choices as to the kind of music and the context in which it is taught – jazz, pop, classical, concerts, operas, competitions, etc.

In the normal functioning of schools, freedom is something we must take for ourselves and not something the school gives us. Indeed schools cannot give anyone freedom it can only be taken by the members themselves. Schools can, of course, restrict freedom but there are limits on what other people can do to us.

Freedom is what we do with the situations in which we find ourselves.

If we are to overcome a sense of being oppressed by a school, a sense of being dominated by an individual or group of individuals, it is necessary to understand the truth about freedom and how it comes about. Freedom cannot be simply handed over for what is given is merely another form of restraint or obligation. The choice must always be made by the one taking freedom not the one who 'gives' it. This concept of freedom is critical in dealing with anxiety and all the bad feelings we have about organizations.

Ultimately it is a question of whose life it is and who is going to create any individual's life for him or her. We sometimes put ourselves into the position of feeling beholden to so many people that we feel we are doing everything for them and nothing for ourselves. But this obligation is of our own choosing – perhaps for deep and complex reasons but nevertheless of our own creation.

Step back and look at your 'obligations'. Compare them with those of other people in a situation similar to your own. Invariably the obligations differ, which proves that they are not in the nature of things but a matter of choice.

The more we feel under obligation to someone, the more we are looking to them to evaluate what we do; we seek approval from them and perhaps reward. It means we have put ourselves under submission to them – not because they require it of us but because something in our own imagination makes us want to do it. We have unilaterally imposed on ourselves a set of obligations and we decide out of our imagination how the other person feels and will react. Since we have created this situation we can unmake it by deciding for ourselves what we really want.

Responsibility

Freedom cannot exist without responsibility and yet many of us want freedom just because we cannot cope with responsibility. Responsibility, like freedom, is still a matter of choice. If we feel a job is burdensome, it is a consequence of the choices we have made in taking on tasks.

> People who are overworked are invariably so because of the choices they have made rather than because the situation is one that forces too many tasks onto them.

A lot of people enjoy being overworked because it makes them feel less guilty (and wanted) and also because it gives them a range of excuses — for instance, for not doing their work as well as they know it can be done. If you want freedom, then you must accept responsibility which in turn means making jobs work for yourself not making yourself a slave to your work.

Sometimes the idea of accountability is raised in this context but accountability is a form of control and coercion. Individuals who behave responsibly obviate the question of accountability since they perform their work in the way they see best and no amount of 'accountability' can change that perception. It is a strange distinction in some people's minds that accountability is the condition of responsibility, whereas it is a matter of control.

Self-control

We are not suggesting that finding and exercising freedom is a painless matter. Becoming free of unnecessary organizational restraints builds up a sense of being in control of ourselves and provides the energy to maintain that condition. We become more and more in control of our world and it becomes increasingly easy to make decisions that centre on our own understood needs. Thus responsibility to ourselves becomes a means of strengthening our emotional response to situations.

Since stress arises out of a sense of not being in charge of ourselves, the greater our sense of self-control the less situations will stress us. Of course, self-regard must be realistic and it is not always easy to be realistic in the confusion of life's complexities but the higher our self-esteem the more realistic we are likely to be. For one thing, high self-esteem allows us to admit to failure and mistakes without bad feelings so we are able to receive feedback from friends and colleagues that helps us towards a realistic reading of circumstances.

> Individuals with low self-esteem may reject comment as unjustified criticism and become immune to realistic advice and assessment. Realism enables us to distinguish between what appertains to ourselves and what is a matter of circumstances.

It is in some ways a little odd that we tend to give a higher value to what others say about us than to what we feel about ourselves. But so long as we get the two in balance, the views of others are necessary in any assessment of the world we work in. It enables a dialogue of exploration.

Nevertheless, it is a persistent factor for many of us that we value more the opinion of certain others than that of those close to us and even our knowledge about ourselves. For many the unattainable object of their careers is to receive approval but they never find it at the level they feel they are at or in the place they are in. They engage in a relentless striving for acknowledgement and praise.

The problem is that there is no certainty that universal approval will ever be attained. For one thing, those who are closest to us and from whom we need it most are unlikely to give it; friends and family are usually sparing with their praise and certainly the first to realize when it is being demanded of them. Furthermore, we usually like friends for reasons other than their achievement (often in spite of it) and see no reason to be continually praising them.

> What endears us to one another is our commonality of failings, our 'ordinariness', our shared humanity.

A strong career orientation is likely to be an unrequited quest. We are in danger of falling into an attachment to what others want of us (or what we think they want of us) rather than doing what is right for us.

Personal fulfilment

Schools being what they are, they can never take full account of individuals and can never be places where we can completely fulfil ourselves. That is why we need to keep ourselves as free as possible from bondage to school organization so that it does not take us over. Such freedom, of course, results from an attitude of mind and is not just the refusing to do the jobs that membership seems to require. In schools people tend to be reduced to a commonality and treated as a commodity so it is necessary for everyone to work hard at recognizing and sustaining individuality.

SUCCESS AND FAILURE OF STUDENTS

It is one of the great paradoxes of schools that while the importance of the individual features highly in the rhetoric the reality often embodies the contrary. Schools often find themselves dealing with students as packages with quality control aimed at grading and classifying not at recognizing uniqueness.

Whatever the administrative reasons for schools being what they are — and administrative reasons always sound plausible — it is odd how the daily life of students can be ordered; age cohorts moving in steady rhythm through the years, work periods rung out by bells, the seasons measured by bouts of assessment, and overall the cataloguing, classifying, measuring and ranking of individuals.

Schools very often seem to be about uniformity and the uniform much more than they are about the individual and the different. The consequence is that each member is more likely to be helped minimally rather than maximally.

Products of the system

What teachers and students learn to do best is to find ways round the system, to turn the defects to personal advantage rather than to exploit the strengths of the school. One of the difficulties with schools is that many of those who go back to teach are successful products of the system in that they come back with all the values that maintain the system and not necessarily those that are essential to reform it. This should mean that they feel at home and at ease but in fact it often means the opposite.

Schools have to change over the years as they adapt to outside needs and pressures and this requires reformist members or at least those who are amenable to change. Many teachers find that schools are changing in ways they do not like and feel that they are out of sympathy with what students now demand. Their difficulty is that it is the needs of students that determine the nature and pace of change not just the wishes of teachers.

Everyone is resistant to change in some way or another and natural caution is essential for well-managed change. If you feel under pressure from prospective change, try to use your resistance positively: not to resist but to modify. You will obtain a greater sense of satisfaction.

Success and failure in school

One of the fundamental difficulties built in to the conventional structure of schools is the assumption that students who present few learning problems are to be most highly valued. Quite often the 'best' teachers are given the cleverest students and the least able are taught by the least academically qualified teachers − though they may be very skilled in working with these particular students.

Many teachers have in their mind's eye a picture of an ideal class of fifteen or twenty highly motivated, hard-working, high-achieving students presenting no disciplinary or intellectual challenge but reflecting glory on the teacher as a competent, warm-hearted pedagogue. Not many envisage the ideal class as one composed of students with emotional, social and intellectual problems who find difficulty in learning and co-operating well together and with whom the teacher has to struggle collectively and individually to help them to achieve. Those who do, find it more satisfying.

Schools tend to reward success and punish failure when it would be more realistic to accept success as reward enough for the successful student and to accept failure as necessary to the process of learning. Teachers should be able to see themselves as being essentially there to help pupils to learn and this means that helping those who find learning difficult is what teaching is all about. When a teacher starts from the wrong premiss and expects teaching to be easy and with obedient pupils, there will inevitably be a sense of frustration, disappointment and depression.

If students are required to do what they do not want to do there is bound to be trouble. Teachers do not overcome this trouble just by being more entertaining, though it may help in a crisis. Lack of involvement in learning is overcome only by providing activities that are meaningful to the students and that the students want to do. Students need to know that a teacher with assist with problems and not expect immediate or even ultimate success.

Improving the quality of relationships

If we change the relationship between teacher and student and if we place the onus of decision-making on the students so that they have to decide what they want to do and to negotiate with the teacher how they might do it, we can take away much of the potential stress from teaching. When a teacher understands that classroom relationships are a matter for continual negotiation they will look for success in the negotiation process rather than what the students can be persuaded to learn.

One way of looking at situations that are stressful to us is to acknowledge that we have become locked into only one way of perceiving them and unless we can see them in another way (and often any other way at all will do) we shall never break out of our restraints. Anyone who is suffering from stress in relationships must renegotiate the relationship.

Teacher dominance

A primary characteristic of schools is the dominance teachers have over students in most material considerations. There are all kinds of evidence of this not least the comfort of the accommodation of teachers as opposed to students. By and large teachers are greatly privileged and students underprivileged though the balance may alter as they grow older; further education colleges tend to be more comfortable than secondary schools and universities are more comfortable than primary schools. (Think of lavatory accommodation in this respect. There are not many teachers who would tolerate the kind of lavatory accommodation that many pupils have to use!)

Schools tend to be dominated by teachers at the expense of students. Teachers also have rights that students do not have. They may withdraw their labour under trade union legislation but students may not. These restrictions on students lead to anger and frustration which are easily and usually turned on the teachers.

Perhaps schools will only change slowly towards providing proper conditions for students but individual teachers can do a lot to make things better. Simply changing our attitude towards student needs, their physical comfort and environment will improve conditions because remedies will be more easily thought of — allowing students into classrooms during break times and sharing time with them perhaps over a drink informally may be one improvement. Even seeing students as 'people' rather than 'children' or youths will lead to an enhanced awareness of need and increase the comfort of solutions.

In practice many teachers want a good deal more than a formal relationship with students and much of the disappointment that teachers experience arises from their hidden expectations. They may well want to get emotionally closer to the students than the formal relationship allows. It is likely that many teachers sincerely want more intimate relationships than teaching usually offers and that is one reason for their sense of underachieving. But the organization of schools makes a change impossible and teachers have to make do with satisfactions of a certain kind, the academic attainment of their students.

UNDERSTANDING STUDENT REACTIONS

Feedback and change

The inability to adapt easily to new circumstances is not confined to schools; many organizations find the same problem. Schools seem to lack the feedback mechanisms that tell them that they are not adapting (e.g. cash flow, market share) and it becomes even more important for them to be sensitive to the sources of information that are readily available which is through the student body in a variety of ways. This can only be done when there is such a relationship between the school (i.e. the teachers) and the students that there is a free flow of information of all kinds and the school (i.e. the membership as a whole) is able to evaluate correctly what is said.

In all organizations whose primary clients are people this open dialogue is essential if frustrations are not to build up. Hospitals are a case in point where patients are often considered to have no part whatsoever in their own diagnosis, care, cure or rehabilitation. If the movement in hospitals is towards closer contact with patients, it must also be necessary for schools to do the same. Without that emotional closeness between partners there can only be an increase in unease.

Teachers often unwittingly invest an enormous amount of energy in buying themselves credits through their students. To the formal credits of examination results and the like they add informal ones such as producing school plays, organizing trips and visits, managing the cross-country team. Then they apply for a promoted post and fail to get it. They are devastated because they really believed someone was counting up their good works and was ready to give out the 'glittering prize'. 'I've done a lot for this school and look what I get!' denotes both disappointment and bitterness.

The question is, Who do we do things for — ourselves or other people? If for ourselves we cannot demand that others recognize us and reward us. If it is for others then we still cannot demand rewards on our terms since those others must be the judges of the worth of what we do. There is a dilemma because teachers are encouraged to work beyond the demands of a basic teaching relationship by all sorts of promises and inducements. But in the last resort we are all left to our own devices and our own sense of reward.

We need to know for whom we are doing things. We do most things for ourselves but sometimes like to think we are being altruistic. But you cannot be altrusitic about your own career and it is dangerous to confuse loyalty with self-interest.

Flexibility and adaptability

Successful schools are characterized by flexibility and adaptability, a considerable openness to a variety of member needs and an openness to new ways of doing things. Many schools tend to be organized as if there were a high level of 'normality' and ignore what can be conveniently labelled *abnormal* or *deviant*. Schools do not usually set out to cater for special needs. Once a group of students has been classified − low attainers, gifted, BTEC, TVEI, CPVE, etc. − it is often considered that all the tasks of special needs have been dealt with. But there are many other kinds of important differences among students (and people), different styles of learning, different personalities and temperaments, different diurnal rhythms of energy, different emotional and intellectual perspectives, and so on.

Another cause of stress is the conflict arising from individual differences and organizational patterns and expectations. The simple pattern of the school day and the school week will be exceedingly stressful to some teachers just because they do not fit into the natural rhythms of the place. They might be quite unaware that this is because of the kind of person they are, not just because they are wilful or incompetent.

Deviance

When the matter of serious deviance arises, schools are seldom able to cope well because deviance is perceived as a fundamental threat rather than an inevitable consequence of organization. One way of dealing with deviance is either to ignore it or to punish it. Whichever solution is adopted it can be made easier to cope with if it is depersonalized or turned into an administrative matter. With highly impersonalized regimes, system maintenance is all important and senior members become preoccupied with trivia and the enforcement of regulations. The boundaries round the organization become tightly drawn, and people are only allowed in on their best behaviour and if they obey the rules which are often extended outwards to repel all boarders.

Schools use school rules in an attempt to obtain objectivity. They are always stoutly defended as 'the minimum necessary for good order', but often concern themselves with such trivia as the wearing of earrings, colour of socks, kind of trousers permitted, time to be spent on homework. These are all intended – unwittingly no doubt – to fend off delinquents before they even recognize themselves but in fact it makes deviants of virtually everyone who comes into the school.

A preoccupation with rules is often a substitute for something else. Quite possibly a teacher who chooses to insist on regulations being adhered to really wants a closer relationship but is afraid of closeness or intimacy.

Not surprisingly, fearing closeness leads to behaviour which prevents it.

Tolerance and acceptance

Among the qualities of personal maturity are tolerance and the ability to accept others for what they are without personal distress. It is easy to laugh at Alf Garnett with his excessive prejudices and be pleased when he has his come-uppance. But for many of us there is just below the surface a breaking point to what we can put up with. We may fear losing control or perhaps we lack confidence but our level of tolerance is determined by the amount of threat we perceive. Fear leads to intolerance, but it is fear of ourselves not the object that induces the fear.

In the practical world of the classroom the fear may be a consequence of low self-esteem. We fear we will not be able to handle a class rather than that they will get the better of us; a subtle but critical difference. This may be why many teachers wish to teach the 'best' classes (that is, the most well-behaved); why certain subjects are looked down upon, why teachers are valued at the level of the subject, and why deviance and misbehaviour are so feared though they are different things. The more secure you feel about yourself the more you will be able to tolerate other people's differences.

PROBLEMS OF CARING FOR STUDENTS

Normalization

A principle for action that is gaining favour in work with deviant groups is that of normalization. This states that people should have access to be the norms of society, to experience normal values rather than being separated from social norms and reinforcing deviant values. The more deviant a group is believed to be the more isolated from the normal they become. For example, there is a false logic to assuming that all students with reading difficulties should be grouped together. They may have little in common even in terms of reading difficulties and they may each learn better from peers who can read well and will certainly not see themselves as labelled *special* (or *deviant*). The pedagogic benefits of segregation are minimal compared with the social benefits of integration.

Pastoral care

Another school system which purports a welfare purpose is pastoral care. Here some pupils do seem to have a choice of opting in to help and are free to approach members of staff for help, advice or support. However, many pastoral care systems operate punitively. As one pastoral head of fifth year said, 'Ask around the school; they think I'm a sod, and that's what I am to them'. Significant people in pastoral care systems take on the role of bogy man for some students, because teachers often use them as threats for what will happen if they get themselves into trouble, which more often than not means if they are disobedient or will not conform. If a student is 'sent for', the usual feeling is of having done wrong and the summons is for punishment.

This is not to deny that many teachers do help and support some students, but it is generally a minority who receive active support without seeking it. Those who do are students who are able to penetrate the mask of authority and see the humanity beneath. Even within this system of caring there is the understanding that the problem lies within the child who is desperate enough to ask for help without acknowledging that the situation has been almost entirely created by the school. Sometimes the cause is attributed to the family in the belief that once a family has been classified as 'difficult' or 'problem' the reasons for a child's behaviour have been explained.

There are many sources of difficulty for students in coping with school not least teachers and particularly those who exercise power without much regard to justice and reason. When attempting to solve problems, pastoral care staff often resort to the 'within child' perspective partly because it is simpler to do that for them but also because of the ethos of the school in emphasizing some differences and ignoring others. It is far more problematic to have to change a timetable, retrain a corps of teachers, be flexible about hours of attendance, than to offer a student personal advice.

One of the major problems for those pastoral care staff who want to change things on behalf of individuals is that they are often swamped by demands to punish other students because most teachers prefer to see problems as being caused by a few deviants rather than being within the general organization of the school – of being a consequence of what the school is rather than of the individual.

Student feedback

Students give clues about themselves but these can be largely ignored or misunderstood by teachers. Teachers enjoy positive feedback from students but any loss of this feedback can lead to stress. Yet students do not give positive feedback unless the teacher delivers the goods. If a class withdraws its positive feedback, the teacher may feel stressed, may feel inadequate but may not understand the implications in terms of human relations or individual responses. Teachers often regard the human interaction part of their job as an additional demand which is all right on occasion, whereas the 'real' job of teaching is getting facts across.

A record sheet or report form (Figure 4, page 86) can be used to analyse problems of individuals – both teachers and students – groups, and organizations. The frequent response of teachers who have used it is to express surprise at how little they knew and this itself is a salutary exercise. Often teachers try to solve problems without any hard facts but with half-truths and rumour. The form can be used in an assessment process to gather information pertinent to solving the problem and thereby make the best estimate about it. It can be reviewed to see if progress has been made and to generate yet more information. It can be used as part of an assessment cycle, typical in its own way of good teaching.

The assessment cycle

Gather information
Formulate hypotheses
Intervene
Evaluate

As can be seen from Figure 4, it is assumed that the same aspects can be both stressful and a resource or source of help. We all know that our close families give us both the most support and the most stress. The complexity of human relationships is emphasized by the form and it shifts the emphasis away from the problem residing within the individual and catalogues the contribution made by other social networks. Coping strategies are seen to result from an interaction of all these factors.

It is often difficult to decide whether a coping strategy is appropriate or not according to whether it is measured by short- or long-term benefits but, for an individual clearly identified by the school as deviant, some strategies will be obviously inappropriate because the escalating nature of the problem will create more and more stress for the individual.

Three types of outcome or intervention strategy are suggested for consideration. If coping strategies result from an interaction of stresses and resources, two separate lines of attack are the removing of the source of stress and increasing resources. They have been written down as changes that can be made and learning needs. They can apply to anyone and also to groups. The third tactic is to consider other strategies – for example, finding out more information. Consider the information provided about 'Simon' in Figure 4.

As can be seen, the information in Figure 4 is patchy. This is typical of the information that is available to teachers. The truth of some of it can be doubted and clearly Simon himself should be involved in the next stage. However, already some possible ways of intervening, or offering help, have been advanced, all of which would furnish more exact information. Indeed, Simon might decide that he does not wish to have any of the help on offer and in particular may see the 'other strategies' as an infringement of his privacy and private life outside school.

The other important point illustrated by Figure 4 is that often more negative information is available to teachers than positive information; teachers often do not know whether any sources of support are available to students. Clearly, within a school setting, the teacher that a student may choose to honour with a request for help may not be the 'official' person for that student's year group, class or house; such contacts may be unknown to the rest of the teaching staff, and may even be ignored by the teacher concerned.

The advantage of writing down, albeit very briefly, this information is that it cuts through the usual way that information is transmitted in school – by anecdote and hearsay. While anecdotes can be useful ways of illustrating points or even conveying information, they do not provide direct and clear information and are unreliable without substantiation. Teacher knowledge of pupils that comes only from classroom conversation is only partial and may even be a long way from the 'real' truth. In Simon's case one might question the truth of the idea that he has few or no close friends and whether this is a source of stress since some people prefer few friends.

Report Form		
	Name *Simon*	
	Stresses	**Resources**
Self	*Poor academic skills, poor self-image.*	*Charming and pleasant.*
Friends	*Few close or good friends.*	*Liked by girls.*
Peers	*Tends to be a bully*	*?*
Family	*Finds both parents difficult to get on with. Father aggressive and mother emotionally unstable. Sister ?*	*?*
School/teachers	*Picked on by teachers (red hair means easily visible)*	*Likes Mr Newcomb.*
System	*Often sent to year head.*	
Community	*Involved in petty crime, but not yet been caught by police*	*Enjoys leisure time, goes to youth clubs*
Coping Strategies		
Changes that can be made	*Offer regular and reliable support in school to listen to problems as they occur and offer help if needed.*	
Learning needs	*Social skills training Vocational guidance Advanced reading course.*	
Other Strategies	*Find out more about peer group relationships. Try to establish links with family (??). Try to establish links with youth club.*	

Figure 4 Example of a report form

Quality of information

The quality of information is a crucial matter in any problem involving stress but especially when there is likely to be clouding as in school situations. There are different levels of information which each have different levels of reliability. We can express them here on a linear scale from very reliable to very unreliable.

Informal Observation and Experience

The first stage of information gathering is unconscious; we are not aware that we are gathering information but become aware that we have done so when we discover an insight into a problem we may have thought new to us. For example, teachers may find themselves wondering whether a particular child has a hearing loss or difficulty in seeing the board from a distance. What has happened is that the teachers will have observed events or happenings over a period of time which have gradually but imperceptibly built up into a picture of that child's behaviour, and detected some unusual aspects of it which clarify into the question of hearing or seeing difficulties. This is the first level of information which is obtained by informal observation and experience.

Rumour and Hearsay

The second stage can be typified by rumour or hearsay. The teacher who has become aware of the 'insight' may approach other colleagues and asks whether they have noticed similar behaviour and if they have an explanation. The speculation then takes on the status of an observation with a tested hypothesis. The second teacher may not have noticed anything amiss but may feel bound to assent or to excuse him- or herself from not having noticed because the nature of teaching is different in their class. If the first teacher is always sharing speculations that subsequently prove to be without foundation, the second teacher may deny that the child has a disability simply through experience of their colleague rather than the child. Informally observed information may thus gain status from the person who gives it rather than from any inherent truth.

Informal Verification

The third stage is an attempt at verification at an informal level. The teacher will now look for situations and events which confirm the insight by informal observation at a conscious level. It is rare for attempts to be made to refute the insight; at this stage the teacher would probably not attempt to test out the insight directly but would rely on naturally occurring events.

An example of this type of behaviour is the cat lover who claims that the cat knows its name. The proof offered is that the cat comes when its name is called. This stage may be further elaborated by consultation with colleagues and the information taken on greater trust than before.

Information Testing

A higher level strategy is employed at the next stage. Here attempts may be made formally to confirm the information by testing. Some tests are designed to refute particular hypotheses. In addition structured observation may be used to test out how the individual will behave in those circumstances.

In schools this stage is more likely to be undertaken by someone other than the class teacher; by a teacher who may be designated a special role in being able to identify certain problems. This teacher may be in the position of the cat lover who calls the cat by another name to see if it responds in the same way. In addition to in-school testers and observers there are the other professionals who take on this role including peripatetic teachers, speech therapists, educational psychologists and clinical medical officers.

Residential Assessment

The ultimate weapon is the residential assessment which claims to provide comprehensive information about individuals. The reason for elaborating all of this is to ensure that problem-solvers are aware of the quality of their information. The aspects that are important are: firstly, the source of the information; secondly, the evidence given to support it; and, thirdly, whether it is pertinent to the problem.

As you proceed, you will be able to find out more information which should improve your original position and confirm or refute parts of it. Human interactions are so complex that it must be expected that misunderstandings will occur. It is quite possible, for example, that a student is not lying but simply presenting his or her understanding of the truth. And the same will be true for the teacher, even if the original assumption is that the one has the better perception of the truth than the other.

Much of the information that is obtained about students in the process of stress problem-solving may be irrelevant to the solution of the particular problem but may make teachers feel that the student has greater problems that require intervention. This is a very problematic area with no clear guidelines for solving matters. Obviously, some knowledge of previous problems must be acted upon (e.g. non-accidental injury or sexual abuse) but others may present real difficulty over whether this knowledge should be shared or kept confidential.

Criteria for evaluation of the information in this case may be very important and this consideration returns us to the three criteria of source, evidence and pertinence. In the collection of information about students, a great deal of anecdotal information will be obtained and it is necessary to consider how pertinent it is.

Sources of information

Problem-solving appears to rely on good information but much experience of schools suggests that not enough effort is made to collect good information. Because of the priorities of tasks and timetabling, problems are often approached on the basis of the need for an instantaneous solution which requires the determination of a suitable punishment.

In some schools speed of decision is synonymous with justice. It is only when problems will not go away that teachers look for a different way of approaching them. The dilemma is often that something 'needs to be done immediately' but the 'solution' that ensues is only an interim solution and not concerned with the real problem. The implication is that no punishment should be given but that a holding action should be taken until matters are properly sorted out.

Contracting

When students have problems that lead to emotional difficulties one solution is to initiate a period of 'contracting'. This is done by the use of specific contracts with students and can be very successful in solving problems on the part of the school, even if it does not go all the way to solving the problems of the student(s) other than by regularizing social relationships. Contracts work best when they truly are contracts laying down the expectations and rights of both parties, and are the result of a negotiated process. They cannot work well when one of the parties is coerced – usually the student – into accepting a contract that is from their point of view undesirable.

A problem of contracts in school is that teachers are often unable to fulfil their commitments not because they do not want to but because the priorities of the school over-ride the teacher's own priorities. 'Free time' when teachers often undertake this sort of task is eroded by the need to undertake additional jobs, such as substituting for colleagues. Consequently, teachers may be seen as people who cannot be trusted and students finds themselves taking defensive action. Students often feel teachers are too busy to give the attention they need and so despair of building up a substantial person-to-person relationship – in fact identifying teachers as people who cannot help them.

5
ORGANIZATIONAL DEMANDS: ADMINISTRATION AND BUREAUCRACY

● Why administration causes stress ● Fear of officialdom ● The tyranny of time ● Making routines useful ● Dealing with meetings ● Expecting too much from others causes stress ● How to be assertive ● The basis for good social relationships

WHY ADMINISTRATION CAUSES STRESS
Relationships among people

Much stress occurs as a consequence of what happens in the school as an organization. As we have said, organizations do not exist apart from the individuals who compose them and the impact of organization is not so much the consequence of 'the organization' as of the perception and response of individuals. For example, some teachers find the writing of termly reports on students — which is an 'organizational requirement' — an irksome chore, while others value the opportunity to communicate with parents about a student in a formal way.

It is not the task itself which is either agreeable or disagreeable but the feelings we have when we do it for reasons that are quite personal.

Criticism from a colleague might hurt but it might also be amusing dependent on how we perceive the colleague. When individuals find a situation stressful they are responding to the way they feel about people not the tasks the people lay upon them.

> It is not the changing of organizational requirements that will make life less stressful but the helping of people to view their relationships with others in the organization differently.

It is important for us to emphasize this view because in this chapter we deal with changes in administrative processes and procedures and their relationship to stress. We believe that matters can be changed for the better by doing them differently but this is largely because the person bringing about the changes sees things differently. In other words, the important condition is that individuals change and take a different view of what they do.

Running meetings

The running of meetings provides a good example. There are a number of good books about how to improve the quality of formal meetings; they all contain advice that will help the meetings to run better and give more satisfaction to the members. But there is a condition that is usually not mentioned and that is the attitude of the chairperson to the meeting, because if their attitude does not change no amount of jiggering around with techniques will make the meetings better. This also applies to the attitudes of members to the meeting and how disposed they are to making it work well.

For example, it is good practice to review the agenda before working through the business with a view to prioritizing items and allocating time for their attention. However, if the chairperson is an authoritarian individual or unusually inept, the new techniques will merely underline and reinforce their normal behaviour. Members may feel unable or unwilling to co-operate simply as a consequence of the personal style of the chairperson.

The purpose of administration

The first thing to remember about administration is that it is intended to be a facilitative process that exists to serve the needs of the members of the school. 'Members' in this context is a group wider in composition than those who identify themselves formally as members because quite a number of people outside the school are effectively members. These subsidiary groups may not be active until there is a crisis, but they have a significant interest in the school and will become involved if there is a threat. Parents may fall into this category but so too will all the school suppliers. Administration has to serve their needs too – the paying of bills, for one thing.

It may be impossible to predetermine the breaking points in the school system. Since administration is merely the routinization of expectations, administrative processes will always have limitations that may become known only after breakdown not before.

> The problem with many administrators is that they actually believe that administrative processes have a validity in their own right and independently of what actually happens in the organization.

Administrative procedures tend to be designed without regard to the people they relate to, which means that they are inherently flawed rather than inherently fault-free as the administrator would believe.

That is not to deny that within their own terms routines work but they are predicated on more secure assumptions about human behaviour than human behaviour actually warrants. Good administrators do not expect administrative systems to work on their own, they allow for human fickleness.

> The best administrators help people to get round administrative routines they do not try to restrict them by petty enforcement.

The impersonality of administration

Many people take administrative positions because they do not like close personal contact with people and because their relationships will be less complicated, more distanced and also more controlling. Some teachers want to be heads because they feel the position will enable them to have more influence over colleagues and be able to control developments in the curriculum better. Some teachers like to move into administrative jobs because they have become disillusioned with class teaching but wish to have greater say in what and how students and teachers do things.

Everyone going into administration hopes that their job will now be more manageable and precise. But administration often makes matters more complicated. There is no escape into 'paper work' and people are no more willing to respond to written requests than spoken ones. For some administrators the opportunity to retreat into paper work is all that they require; it is excuse enough. But many administrators need the paper work to support their fantasy that they will have greater control and are distressed when they find they are no more able to manage their colleagues on paper than they were face-to-face.

Administrators can become very distressed when the administrative tasks fall foul of human reaction and are not the mechanical success they were designed to become. Experienced administrators come to accept the limitations; it is the novice or part-time administrators who find the reality difficult to deal with.

The most effective administrators are those who see themselves as 'servants', whose role is to serve not control.

The perceptual problem is that many see administration as promotion and therefore a superior position. Contrary to much conventional career advice, good administrators should like people and be good at handling them. It is only those who really hold backroom jobs who can afford not to care for relationships with people in their job — though there are few jobs where we can dissociate ourselves entirely from people.

On the whole, good teachers will be bad administrators in the traditional view of administration and will make poor bureaucrats because they have a basic preference for people. When teachers consider administration it is usually a form of escape — say from ambiguity to hoped-for certainty. If they do make such a move, they experience a high level of dissatisfaction. Some teachers do not have a strong need for close contact and they adopt an instructor attitude to students. For them what is taught is much more important than who is taught; their exasperation comes when students do not react as automatically as they would like and they find this stressful.

Effective administrators, like effective teachers, make a basic assumption that their clients will try their best to circumvent even their best effort.

Manipulation and administration

Administration provides a means of manipulating people and almost always someone will feel manipulated even if there is no such intention. A great deal of manipulation is unconscious but nonetheless real. The timetabling of staff provides an ideal opportunity to pay off old scores but sometimes even trying to be scrupulously fair leads to injustice. Some administrators enjoy the degree of control they have simply because it makes people uncomfortable. There is nothing more insidious than getting at someone through a supposedly impersonal procedure.

Coercion by administration

Unquestionably, school organization uses administration to put people in their places. For example, newcomers always get the worst jobs to do, simply because as newcomers they have no established rights and have not negotiated a more favourable position. Most organizational punishment comes through administrative ploys. 'We need someone reliable to look after the table tennis team now that Mr Jones has left. I am sure this is just the job for a man like you with your sort of interests. You don't look after any other teams do you?' The implication here is that the job is light in some way and a fair share of responsibilities is in order. There is an implied shortfall in job capacity.

We may also use administration to fight running battles with colleagues. John Smith can become a continual irritation to Hilda Jones over her weekly absentee returns just because the two of them do not get along well together. The head may find the head of science to be an arrogant person, so the latter is given all the nasty jobs of stock-taking that no one else will volunteer for. We all try to do this by using our influence in administration to pay back old scores in an impersonal way.

Many of us will go to some lengths to settle scores if there is half a chance particularly if we feel we have been badly done to. Where we cannot, or will not, do this alone we will often gang up on someone — especially someone in authority — to get back at the individual. There is the peculiar belief that when you hold a senior position your status of itself defends you from feeling personally attacked. It is as if high position gave high immunity from personal feelings.

> We all seek collective scapegoats. The more commonly they are identified, the less the individual experiences a sense of guilt.

> But scapegoats, by definition, suffer for what is really our own fault. If we could accept responsibility for ourselves neither we nor the scapegoat would suffer.

We see administrative demands as being centrally about someone else and something else, while organization requires the organizer's involvement in a continuing and critical way. Organizing means getting things done through yourself while administration means getting things done through someone else. Administrative chores usually have no immediate or specific pay off for either the administrator or the administered and so tend to be alienative even when there is likely to be a longer-term pay off.

Coping with administrators

> There are three ways of dealing with other people's requirements of us:
> One is to ignore them and hope they will go away.
> The second is to respond fully and conscientiously.
> The third is to deal with them expeditiously but without regard to whether our response is correct or not.

Most administrators are so pleased to receive an immediate response that they will forgive any faults and make the corrections themselves. Nothing annoys an administrator more than delays. The way in which we respond depends on the kind of person we are and our habitual response pattern. But this causes a lot of people worry because they feel a sense of guilt even if they stubbornly refuse to accede to demands.

> Many of us are in some way afraid of administrators because they are authority figures, and we hold authority figures in awe.

Perhaps teachers are prone to this fear because they work in an environment that has all the associations of their own childhood and the same authority relationships exist that they knew as students. But almost everyone feels some anxiety when dealing with bureaucracies and our fears are reinforced because bureaucrats work at an impersonal distance from us.

FEAR OF OFFICIALDOM

Our experience of organizations is less impersonal than we sometimes claim. Since we cannot relate to any organizations or any form of administration without doing it through a person, it is specific experiences of people that colour our view of organizations either specifically (where we can identify a person) or generally (where we transfer our experience from one organization to another). A pro forma that comes to us from a colleague might be delayed because we see no urgency but one from the head might be filled in at once because we have a sense of his or her authority. The situation might be reversed for the same reasons; the colleague is close but unthreatening while our delay in returning the form to the head is a way of asserting our independence.

Perceptions of authority

For some people the mere impersonality of a communication from an 'official' of any kind is a cause of fear and some people are terrified of a letter or note from the boss. It can be quite disconcerting to receive a note from the head which says 'Would you be good enough to call in and see me', or something even more cryptic! Many of us assume that such ambiguous messages bode a rebuke – remember what it was like being called to see the head when we were school children?

Indeed it is wise for heads always to make clear why communications are sent and why a colleague is requested to call in on them. The better practice is for heads to call in on colleagues in the common room or classroom as a matter of course.

> The concept of the open door to the head's room has a sinister meaning when the head never comes through it.

THE TYRANNY OF TIME

Perceptions of time

One of the most misunderstood elements in our life is time and the use we make of it. It is generally considered that time is a matter entirely outside our control and a quantity that we can 'waste' or 'lose'. Undisputably there is 'clock time' which is measured in a way accessible to most of us but that is only one aspect of time; time is essentially an experience and that means that we all experience time differently.

It is this difference of experience which is the key to a beneficial understanding of time. Many of us use our own perception of time as a stick to beat other people with; we justify many of our demands on others by specifying some timescale but we fail to realize this is our own timescale and not necessarily applicable to them.

> Some people experience anxiety by projecting their own time perspective onto other people.

One trouble with schools is that they seem to be organized as if time were the only real consideration. Because time plays so large a part in the administration of a school, time issues become dissipated into almost every activity. What we need to ask continually is, What meaning in time terms do our demands have upon one another?

For instance, the basic assumption that learning is related to the time allocated by school is entirely questionable. Schools talk of 'late developers' as if there were an inherently 'correct' timescale for learning. How late is late? And how early would early be? Can development be 'late' and 'early'? How does one person determine early and late for another?

> Schools often use time as a means of laying onto the students some of the problems that are unresolved among the teachers − unresolved issues of quality in the curriculum, for example.

Changing our view of time

One way of manipulating time and forcing a single view of it onto other people is through the routines that administration demands in order to function properly. An administrator thinks of time as a piece of material of limited dimensions that has to be cut up into manageable pieces − length being more important than quality.

The school year is saturated by measured time and minutes are often more important than hours. Teachers are taught to plan their lessons minute by minute, while the school year has three great swells of time punctuated by a staccato of breaks. The school year ploughs on regardless of what people do and the events that crowd their lives outside the school.

Routines

For most people a degree of routine is helpful and civilized life as we know it could not proceed without the underpinning of routine. But we continually find these routines frustrating — like Sunday bus services. Good administrators make routines work for them but bad administrators try to make everyone else work to the routine.

We all need to examine our myths about routine and time if we are not to become totally subordinated to artefacts of our imagination that no longer serve our needs. We should look carefully at our routines and try to find out what they mean to us, what kind of security they offer and what sorts of restraint. For example, we need to look at our views of deadlines.

It is easy to become anxious because tasks have been left until the last minute, but if we do this habitually the question is not whether we ought not to so leave them but, Do we fail to get them done in the end?

So long as we catch the deadline there seems no reason why leaving things to the last minute shouldn't continue to work for us. Only if it doesn't work do we need to look at what we do with our time.

For some people procrastination is just the way they work while for others getting jobs done at once is their way; neither is better than the other because it follows from their personal experience of time.

Being aware of how we create our personal deadlines is important if we are to free ourselves from unnecessary anxiety. Most students leave their weekend homework to the last minute on Sunday night or even Monday morning and experience varying degrees of guilt about it; or just annoyance at the discomfort. Most of us have had this experience. What we were in fact doing was working to our own personal deadline but laying constraints upon ourselves that came from someone else's deadlines. So long as we did what had to be done by the time it was needed it did not matter when (or even how) it was done. Yet we may have felt that it was somehow more 'proper' to do the work on Friday night and get it out of the way. This all sounds very much as if we have taken some precepts from our parents to heart and are laying a criterion of their convenience on to our own practice and inclination.

MAKING ROUTINES USEFUL

Personal routines

Personal routines, on the other hand, can assist us in avoiding stress. If we clean our teeth twice a day we are saved the anxiety of dental decay. If we want to be able to put on a clean shirt each day, we have to ensure that our dirty clothes are washed at the correct time. If we have our car serviced regularly we hope to be spared the unexpected engine problem.

But some anxiety in even ordinary matters is part of our enjoyment for we seem to be habitual in those routines that cause us some concern. Always being on the last minute for a train or bus, always volunteering to do jobs we later regret, always using credit cards to make excess purchases – these are all examples of habitual behaviour that cause some people considerable and often continuous low-level anxiety. Most actors suffer some form of stage nerves and mountain climbers usually experience fear yet they all persist in apparently stressful activities. It is more than likely that we feel more in charge of ourselves and/or the situations when we have survived our anxiety – and may even enjoy it!

DEALING WITH MEETINGS

Making formal meetings work for us

Considering how almost universally disliked most formal meetings are it is a wonder they are ever called. Yet within schools we persist in calling one another to these dreadful events. It may be that many of us actually like to be bored and annoyed by inept chairpersons and loquacious colleagues, but at least they give us something to complain about and they make our own work appear a model of efficiency by comparison.

Fortunately, there are quite a lot of ways of dealing with meetings both as an organizer and a member. They can be made much more satisfying but an important question is why we do not try to improve them more than we do. The reason is probably that few of us take them at their face value. They are in fact symbolic representations of all the underlying conflicts in the organization in which they occur, but they play out the conflicts very gently at a surface level and merely confirm the power structure that exists.

Meetings formally and visibly establish who is who and what is what but they are seldom occasions for bringing about change. That is why most of us leave matters as they are and only the foolhardy try to use them as arenas for creating change through head-on confrontation. A lot of people with a desire to reform an organization choose to do so in the formal meeting structure only to be frustrated by their lack of success.

Formal meetings are highly ritualized occasions for acting out set pieces and party pieces; the tune is played and the members dance on cue. The best advice for most of us is to attend only as many meetings as is necessary for our job performance and to restrict our commitment to the strictly necessary.

It is worth remembering that meetings themselves never decide anything though some people who are at a meeting may well do; but what they decide has to be determined by events rather than statements. A large number of decisions supposedly taken in formal meetings are later 're-negotiated' often very significantly. Whether one is bound by the decisions taken in a meeting depends very much on one's position in the power structure.

There are always at least two questions about formal meetings:

1. Would the decision have been made even if there had been no formal meeting?
2. To what extend do I feel bound by a decision which only other people were involved in making?

Some people may find the advice largely to ignore formal business mettings to be itself stressful. They may feel very committed to this aspect of organization and management. Perhaps a good deal of their security comes from attending meetings and responding to the decision-making process. In such a case they should continue to do what is least stressful to them.

It may be that we are comfortable in the rituals of meetings just because we have not questioned them and are simply postponing the time when what goes on in them becomes an organizational issue.

It is possible to be so disillusioned that we prefer untroubled routines because we do not have the energy to deal with live issues.

Effective meetings are essentially democratic in that they involve all members according to their relevance. Meetings that ignore the interests of members can lead to the creation of circumstances that cause stress to individuals and to their distancing themselves from further involvement. That is one reason why majority decisions are to be avoided since they put the minority at a severe disadvantage. Majority vote-taking may be more authoritarian than benign dictatorship.

EXPECTING TOO MUCH
FROM OTHERS CAUSES STRESS

False expectations

Organizations are, as we have said repeatedly in various ways, what we make them; they are creations of our imagination over and above the material substance they may have. We are inclined to endow them with characteristics and qualities that orginate only in our imagination and which cannot be inherent in the system itself. By and large we expect too much of school organization, especially those parts for which we are not responsible ourselves.

> What we so often do is have expectations of other people that are less than reasonable because they arise out of a frustration with ourselves and our inability to cope; so we expect someone else to do it for us. Since other people are likely to disappoint us, a sure way to avoid stress through frustrated expectations is to expect little from other people.

In schools heads are the focus of most of these projected expectations. We expect heads to be pleasant and smiling every time we go to them. We charge in like a bear with a sore head and expect to be greeted by sweetness and light when we tell the head that 5C is rioting. We expect the governors to recognize our worth and importance not to say contribution to the general well-being of the school and to offer the promotion we know we so richly deserve. We expect parents to know how hard we work with their offspring and lavish every care and attention on them treating them even better than they are at home. We expect neat and tidy work from our students every time we set difficult tasks; and so on. All these expectations arise out of our own view of the world not that of the people we work with.

Self-esteem and valuing others

There seems to be a close relationship between how we value ourselves and how we value other people. If we have high self-esteem our expectations of other people are flexible and modest. If we do not think highly of ourselves then we expect too much or too little of others depending on whether we are in high or low spirits. Those who feel bad about themselves usually expect to be treated badly by others. The more highly we value ourselves the more likely we shall perceive others in a positive way.

> The successful way to overcome the anxieties of expectations is to accept more responsibility for ourselves and take charge of changing circumstances by changing our perception of them. It is always worth trying to do this in the classroom because some of the students will respond quite rapidly to being treated differently.

The effect of depersonalization

Because we try to make organizations more impersonal than they are, we forget that they are only made up of people like ourselves. One effect of this is to lead us to attribute qualities to a person in a position as if they were an endowment of the organization rather than qualities of the person. Thus we expect heads to have wisdom, insight, magnanimity, etc. because of their position and irrespective of their having these qualities personally.

Heads may hope that they automatically acquire the qualities of headship on being appointed to the post. Of course, qualities attributed to a position are likely to be evident simply because people see what they wish to see and groups of people collude with one another to reinforce commonly desired characteristics, but in the long run there is a reality testing that begins to break through the collective illusions; the only trouble is that it may take a very long time.

> The individual teacher who is troubled by the behaviour of colleagues, at whatever level, can take consolation that there is nothing superhuman about them but that they are behaving just like anyone else and are no less formidable than they would be in the local pub.

Coping with demands

The key factor in helping yourself in a school is to try to understand the kinds of expectation there are and to work within them. This may require the use of good social skills to negotiate and effectively bring about changes for your own benefit.

One way of bringing about improvement in your social skills is to follow the guidelines of assertion or assertiveness training. This does not mean being aggressive or pushy but rather the putting firmly your own point of view.

> One principle of self-assertion is that you should be true to yourself and try to get what you want without infringing another person's rights or dignity.

We can all think of people who get their own way (at least, that is what we assume) by bullying others, steam-rollering everyone else's wishes and being very difficult to live with if they don't win. These people may have an excessive sense of competitiveness that leads them into behaviour which spoils their relationships with others by exacting concessions that are resented.

There are different styles of behaving which may be at the extreme ends of the continuum of being either exceedingly aggressive or entirely submissive. Aggressive people might get their own way at the time but may be ignored when when they are not actually present. This sort of behaviour also breeds resentment, frustration and anger since reason appears to be wasted on someone who wants to dominate.

The opposite sort of person is equally frustrating and in turn is likely to feel frustrated, hurt and put upon. The overly submissive person is overaccommodating and does not want to upset anyone. Such a person will not complain and can be infuriatingly vague when asked what they would like to do. If people do get angry, as they are bound to do, with the subordinate types there is a great deal of upset and hurt because their intentions were honest, but they are doormats and quite soon they suffer from being almost entirely ignored. These types of extreme are described as stereotypes but they are within everyone's experience.

We all know of colleagues who are so aggressive no one will associate with them even on professional business and most schools have someone whom everyone walks over. But it is worth considering whether this behaviour isn't reactive and fulfilling a need of the staff in general.

> Sometimes we gain acceptance by becoming the scapegoat everyone needs.

Problems of self-esteem

There are a number of dispositions which can take extreme forms; one of these is modesty. In Western society, modesty is taken as virtuous and we do not unduly sing our own praises. But we may so undervalue ourselves that we engage in false modesty. We may, of course, have a genuine and excessive modesty but we may also be hoping for more praise by pretending to a modesty we do not have. We may use it to play 'hard to get' or improve our chances of later support. But our false modesty may have the opposite effect. We may have the skills others praise us for but if we claim that we do not we may lose out altogether.

A second problem disposition is the belief that others can in some way read our minds and know what we want. Much of the time we go around giving hints as to the sort of things that give us pleasure and that we would like to have more of. We do it around Christmas time or birthdays and usually think we have been quite clear about our likes and dislikes. Then we get the very gifts we do not want and this can hurt us a great deal. We may then complain that we had made our wishes quite clear only to be told that we had not been clear enough at all.

Many of us are also deceitful about our feelings and do not answer questions openly. This means that we have no right to be hurt when our feelings are ignored or trodden on. We cannot expect our friends and colleagues to have second sight. And we should be careful not to complain when our secrecy rebounds on us.

A related problem is that sometimes we are deceitful about what we feel when people ask us. Obviously in fleeting contacts one answers according to the situation – you don't go into health details when an acquaintance asks how you are. But when we are asked for our feelings and views and do not give them, we cannot blame others for not taking them into account. Other people can only know what we feel and want if we tell them. We all know people who display bad temper and when asked what is wrong reply, 'Nothing'.

Another relationship that can set up unrealistic demands is the reciprocity of friendship. Briefly, this means that if a friend asks a favour you are unable to refuse because of friendship. But you are also unable to ask a favour unless you are owed one. So, regardless of need, rules are employed to protect the friendship but rules which can actually endanger it since resentment may set in. If I do your class substitution because I am your friend, I may feel resentful because I had earmarked that time for something else of greater personal importance and priority. If you were not my friend I would have refused because of its high priority; however, since I am your friend I owe you the obligation and therefore put myself to considerable inconvenience to accommodate you. Perhaps strangely, the myth of obligation is the opposite of what most people would argue is important in friendship, being able to be oneself.

HOW TO BE ASSERTIVE

Assertiveness defined

How can you be more assertive? The first step is to be more open and honest. If someone asks a question answer it straight without excuses. But take care not to impugn anyone else or reflect on their dignity. Speak only about yourself, your feelings, your opinions. For example, if a colleague has upset you by appearing to damage your classroom authority, it would be more assertive to tackle that colleague by saying, 'I felt upset today when you came into my class. I felt that you undermined my authority. I would prefer it if you spoke to me first before saying anything to the students.' The opposite − personalized blame − would not get you very far and would simply lead to a defensive argument.

> The key to assertiveness is not to personalize issues onto someone else. Identify that part of the problem that is yours and concentrate on your own feelings and thoughts.

The same principle applies to making complaints to organizations. If you put your experience clearly as a problem they are creating for you, they will be more likely to respond positively than if threatened with accusations. The trick is not to blame the other party; this means they have no cause to be defensive.

Self-assertiveness is characterized by positive thinking not negativism. It is that which gives it its strength. It is often easier to be negative and condemnatory but it becomes dually counter-productive; you are less satisfied and the other person becomes more annoyed. It is much easier to get other people to do what you want them to do by putting forward solutions and suggestions that involve yourself than by destructive criticism, however well-informed. Criticism often carries the assumption that the critic feels no responsibility for what has occurred and this make those criticized even more obdurate.

Responsibility for yourself

Taking responsibility for yourself is important and is part of being self-assertive, positive and confident. This also includes taking responsibility for mistakes and being able to apologize without demeaning yourself. Apologies should not be demeaning and should be genuine. We have all been irritated by the insincere apology made as a matter of form only to enable social intercourse to proceed.

An example of this is the way students are instructed to apologize as a ritual to gain re-entry to the classroom; often they do it with a grin and an ironic tone in their voice! Apologies should not be humiliating in any way. We can often apologize for aspects of our behaviour for which we are genuinely sorry even though we may feel totally justified in associated matters. It is only the strong and self-confident person who is able to apologize properly.

In schools it is an aspect of the power structure that teachers do not apologize to students. Administrators also often feel that they are always right and therefore have no need to apologize.

Other aspects of self-assertion are ways of defending yourself against others who do not respect your rights and dignity. We need to be able to stand up for ourselves and can do so by being straightforward in our responses. If asked to do something we do not want to do, it is better to say so than find excuses. We may give reasons but it should not be necessary since it is our intention not to do what is asked that is the issue.

A technique called *Broken Record* can be used. This means repeating the intended message continually until the person addressed has understood and accepted it. If there seem to be unresolved questions about the matter and you feel explanations would be helpful, then an offer to discuss things at another time can be made, but so far as you are concerned the matter is finished.

There are two behaviours which should be avoided. They are responding to implicit criticism and responding to 'red herrings'. Children are very good at offering red herrings which detract from the issue at hand but bosses are equally good at it when they do not want to face unpleasant facts.

Negotiating

So, the key aspects of assertiveness are being positive, being open, taking responsibility for yourself, and having realistic expectations of other people. These, as well as other professional skills, are all factors in negotiating. The good negotiator will enable others to express themselves in terms of their needs and can then operationalize them into possible action outcomes with benefits for all concerned, without anyone feeling that their rights and dignity have suffered.

Professional social skills refer to that range of social skills which are seen to be important for professionals — in our case, teachers. The professional skills needed by teachers include negotiating skills, ability to liaise with others, leadership, consultancy skills, and counselling skills. All these are needed to deal effectively with the wide range of people in addition to students who relate to the school. Generally speaking, this implies that teachers need to be able to negotiate since most of these relationships involve some form of bargaining. The assertive person is always able to negotiate better.

The assertive person can pitch the level of conversation appropriately. Frequent misunderstandings arise because a professional does not realize that a different level of discourse is required in dialogue with a non-professional. The conversation takes place unequally and the non-professional may respond in an aggressive way through feeling disconcerted.

The assertive person is aware of the verbal and non-verbal signals they are sending and can emphasize messages by ensuring that the verbal and non-verbal are in accord, thus saving the hearer from confusion.

The assertive person does not feel self-protective and so will be more able to change behaviour to fit the responses of others. Many difficult situations can be avoided by a quick but effective change of style when a relationship appears to be going badly.

THE BASIS FOR GOOD SOCIAL RELATIONSHIPS

Two important aspects of social relationships are knowledge and skills. It would be pointless to be highly skilled in liaison work and yet not have the knowledge specific to the area in which the work takes place. Similarly, knowledge without skills is useless because there is no way of applying it. It follows that a successful change in a situation requires that both the appropriate knowledge and skills are available to those involved.

However, sometimes only one party in a situation has the requisite knowledge and skills. This is often the case with parents who may not understand how the school works and are unable to find the right staff to deal with. Teachers often find themselves acting as guides and consultants between colleagues and parents trying to bring together appropriate questions and those who can give appropriate answers.

When collating information, it is also important that you do not see what is readily available as the only information about the situation and that it represents the only truth. If you become locked in this sort of mental set it will impair your ability to negotiate by making you rigid and unable to see anyone else's viewpoint. It will nearly always be the case that someone else will have additional information which might completely change the meaning of all the information so far available or considered.

Other people – colleagues, parents, other professionals – all have different information which can change the meaning of our knowledge. In negotiating, it is therefore important to listen carefully to ensure that you have understood the import of what is said.

Listening skills

After listening we should check out on what we have heard by repeating back what we think has been said. We may do this by summarizing or paraphrasing or rephrasing the argument.

If there is a problem of understanding, you can centre the difficulty on yourself rather than blaming the other person for not being clear.

By admitting the difficulty is yours, you make it easier for the other person to restate their point of view.

Much information is conveyed by anecdote and it often takes over a different quality of information exchange. The information you need may be parcelled out in a variety of forms and you may have to listen to several things at a time or over a period of time to get the true message. This is almost certainly going to be the case with a difficult and entrenched personal problem or some sudden personal crisis in an area such as marriage that is not in the public domain. But quite often in a relationship it is enough simply to listen carefully; explanations and further help may not be required. One of the social benefits of assertiveness training is just this ability to listen to others without being judgemental.

Many of us feel we make our worst blunders in liaison, negotiation or counselling by ignoring or being ignorant of information. That is one reason why teachers want personal information about their students so that they can better understand why they behave as they do.

One teacher recalls that he was getting on well with a 'difficult' student until he unguardedly called him 'son' when the reaction was one of considerable antagonism. He subsequently discovered that the boy's father was dead and that the boy felt very badly about it. Of course, we can never have all the information that might be needed and 'mistakes' like this will happen from time to time. In the event, we can avoid showing embarrassment and give a neat, straightforward apology or explanation.

6
HELPING YOURSELF

● Putting yourself first ● Examinations cause stress ● Organizational pressures in the classroom ● Personal satisfactions from school ● Coping with moods ● Techniques for managing our emotional well-being

PUTTING YOURSELF FIRST

This is not a book about the management of schools but about how to cope with them. It is subversive in the best sense because its aim is to help you to get the better of school organization from the standpoint of being an interested party.

Obligation and altruism

Most of us have a strong sense of obligation to others. We unselfishly believe we should not let others down. But how do we know that self-interest and the interests of others are incompatible? We must surely discuss matters before placing ourselves under a restraint. We may simply be reinforcing a double restraint. There is a danger of self-deceit. Sometimes people say, 'I am not doing this for myself, you know; I'm doing it because you need me to.' It must be doubtful if such altruism really exists; it sounds more like doing something for yourself.

After all there is nothing wrong in doing anything because we want to but we have no right to do something for someone else if they do not want us to. We cannot make decisions for other people. The only satis-factory way of dealing with self-interest and our sense of obligation is to ask, 'Is this what I would like for me?' or 'How would I feel in this situation?' We may be wrong in our answer but at least we have not made a higher justification than there really is.

The only way of making certain that 'the school' does not get the better of you is to make certain that you know what you want from the school and that you are going to get it. Of course you may not easily know what you want — most people don't — so the first thing to do is find out.

> If the school were to exist for you and you alone, what would you want? What kinds of reward from life are you looking for and how can the school provide them?

By being unclear about what we want from other people and organiza-tions we send ambiguous messages to those around us. We don't know what we want and they don't understand what we're doing. Not knowing what you want from your circumstances is a sure way of experiencing stress because you have no satisfactory means of evaluating what happens to you. This is by no means as selfish as it may sound.

Unless I go for what I believe is right for me I cannot relate satisfactorily to others. For example, teachers who really love their subject and know that it takes priority over social education will be much more effective teachers than those who pretend that social education comes first but who really only enjoy the content of the subject taught. Since schools have different emphases with regard to 'subjects' and 'social education' it is essential to know which preference you have in accepting a position.

Many teachers have not become aware of the reasons they have for being teachers of certain kinds of student and certain kinds of subject. It is not always that they have a straightforward rapport with people younger than themselves; sometimes there are repressed reasons and for some people the situation is potentially dangerous. Someone who is inadequate in relations with adults would be ill-advised to work with children in the hope that matters will be easy there. Anyone with a grudge against their own teachers would be wrong to believe the system can be changed simply by going back as a teacher. Just occasionally a teacher has a perverse interest in young people that is potentially emotionally damaging. Of course, we enter teaching in the first place because we prefer it to the available alternatives, but it is useful to know why it is an attractive profession to us.

Reasons for teaching

In deciding to go into teaching we all had a lengthy experience of schools. For almost all of us have more experience of schools than any other job (except for those who had experience of farming or lived over the shop). So we take more of our past with us into teaching than almost anyone does into any other profession. There are four kinds of experience that we take with us and all are deeply embedded in our consciousness.

The first is being a pupil and student. This will carry a mixture of likes and dislikes, good memories and bad ones. Some go into teaching because their experience was so good they want to recreate it for others. Some because it was so bad they want to improve things for the new generation. Most of us have experienced a mixture of both.

The second kind of experience is of the patterns and models of teaching and schooling we went through ourselves. We all model ourselves in some way on what we consider our best teachers and we tend to imitate roles that we have enjoyed.

The third is the habituation our own schooling taught us. This includes all the assumptions we make about being a teacher, about schooling and its organization, and about education. It provides us with a very strong sense of continuity especially in terms of the culture of the school, but it may lead to considerable frustration and talking at cross-purposes when in conversation with parents and governors whose experience and sense of continuity are different from ours.

The fourth experience that we bring is of the status of being a student and its relationship to that of a teacher. For many teachers, the experience of being a student in status terms is a long one – perhaps as long as twenty years, certainly no less than fourteen. As teachers they suddenly find themselves in the dominant position. For some this may mean an opportunity to settle vicariously old scores but for most if will lead to an uncertainty in the relationship with older colleagues and those in generally senior positions.

Not infrequently, teachers revert to the role of senior students in their relationship with other adults rather than levelling with them adult to adult. Some teacher behaviours outside school are a replaying of classroom behaviour but its inappropriateness can be confusing to those who are not teachers.

Fulfilment

Teaching like any other job must provide a high level of fulfilment and satisfaction if it is to be well done. If you do not enjoy teaching after a reasonable period of time you should consider giving it up; certainly if the bad feelings persist after a change of schools. After all, there is no reason for doing anything unless it is either enjoyable or necessary. To do anything for a long period that does not provide satisfaction is to put yourself at risk of stress. There are enough circumstances in life when we have no choice − a sick relative, personal ill-health, financial disaster, etc. − so we owe it to ourselves that where we do have a choice the rewards should be highly acceptable to us. If they are not we will stop doing the job as well as it needs to be done.

EXAMINATIONS CAUSE STRESS

Mutual interests of teachers and students

In the end teachers and students have much the same complex of interests − to get along together. However, teacher needs have come to take dominance and in a practical sense they exist more for the teachers than the students so far as structure is concerned. Quite rightly, schools provide career opportunities for teachers and a steadily increasing (albeit small) increase in income. For some teachers the parallel career structure of the examination system has become important and public examinations seem to dominate many secondary schools but comparatively few primary schools.

Public examinations and stress

In many ways a national examination system is hard to justify since it puts the interests of local students below those of students considered nationally. It takes away the freedom of the school to reward students for what they do in the school rather than for what they do in comparison with national norms and it leads to teachers being valued most for their students' examination results.

Public examination systems are bound to create stress and it seems foolhardy to create stress-inducing systems and then be surprised when stress results. Schools have put themselves in a double bind over examinations. We are here only concerned with the effect they have in inducing stress on both teachers, students − and also parents. Schools do not adequately consider the effects of examinations in the creating of stress and they are woefully inadequate in providing assistance for dealing with it.

If a teacher finds teaching a particular class too stressful he or she should ask for another class. And if there is no one willing to do so then the school must face up to the problem that it has allowed to develop. If teachers feel it an indignity or an admission of failure that they cannot cope with a class, the question must be asked as to what is the quality of understanding among teachers that has led to such a situation; one value system for the students and another for the teachers?

The point is that students should be supported in their learning and that means in their mistakes and failures. This is the fundamental basis for fostering learning and the development of responsibility. Teachers also learn and do so by failure and they need the same sort of support as their pupils. You cannot give one kind of support to students and the obverse of it to your colleagues.

We have criticized the public examination system as being inherently stressful yet for some teachers and students it is not so; indeed it is the reverse giving a sense of purpose, certainty and direction. It is from these responses to the public examination system that some of its justification comes. The question is whether for such people it is by chance or design that they feel differently; and would they feel differently if they had a free choice?

ORGANIZATIONAL PRESSURES IN THE CLASSROOM

One of the difficulties of school organization is that choices are severely limited in almost all ways. This may not be a fault in itself but it may conflict with the declared value system of the school as a place where people learn to make choices. In practice, schools may not help students to make good choices because the possibilities on offer are too limited. Generally speaking the making of choices within a school is of a very low level and this is a cause of frustration on the part of many students and not a few teachers.

At even a superficial level choice is limited. The pattern of periods and lessons, breaks and assembly is relentless for teachers and students alike but more for the teacher than the student. Students can coast through the day but teachers cannot because they must provide stimulation throughout the day to a variety of classes and individuals. Both teachers and students have little choice as to how they organize their day and such lack of freedom frequently builds up to considerable frustration.

Perhaps this is one of the major causes of fatigue among teachers; they really have very little freedom of choice during the day and can almost never 'switch off' for a few moments if they feel exhausted or under the weather. Teachers seem to be forced into a working pace that few people would want to keep up in other circumstances. Yet this driving of themselves ahead of the students is by no means necessary.

Because the pressures of the day are so relentless, teachers should ensure a relaxed atmosphere in the classroom. Allow a settling-in period at the beginning of a lesson and a packing-up period at the end.

Organizational restriction

We, all of us, adapt in some way to the school organization that we belong to. We behave somewhat differently in each school according to how we believe we are expected to behave. Of course, these 'expectations' are very personal and originate for the most part in ourselves rather than in the school. All schools will tolerate a considerably greater variety of behaviour than each member believes. We tend to set our own limits rather than have them set for us. This is not to suggest that there are no limits to behaviour because indeed there are, but the limits depend on status of membership; older members and more senior members both assume and are given wider limits on their behaviour than are the new members and junior ones.

Even beyond 'organizational' limits there is variation in personal limits. Some of us cope well with the restrictions and others cope badly. One teacher may find extreme irksomeness where another finds sweet reasonableness but most of us adapt reasonably well. Perhaps it is important to recall that for the most part what one individual will consider a crime of great enormity others will show little concern for.

When we find ourself in conflict with the 'organization' of the school, we do well to consider how much is of our own making; it is more than likely that any confrontation originates in ourselves rather than having its provenance elsewhere and we need to know why we want it. The longer we stay in them the better we cope. After all conflict is nearly always avoidable if we wish it to be so.

Because other people make demands on us in schools, we find ourselves responding to expectations — or what we believe to be expectations — in ways that often put us under the stress of pleasing others. Sometimes these demands seem to require us to do things we do not wish to or about which we have strong feelings; demands which may conflict with our self-defined role. We may feel some of the demands expose our weaknesses — weaknesses we are ashamed to have — and we become anxious about our performance.

English teachers may feel they are expected to take an interest in school drama even though they themselves have no inclination that way. To show willing, however, they agree to produce school plays but the production turns out to be less successful than they would like. Consequently they have a sense of public failure. Similarly geography teachers may feel they ought to be organizing field trips though their domestic circumstances make it very difficult; as a consequence they feel inadequate as geography teachers. In both cases the origin of the pressure would lie in the teachers themselves though there would also be support from others in the school who accepted the definitions of the job provided by the teachers who felt under stress.

Although the pressures are self-defined they have a validity in that they can be confirmed from observation of other people's behaviour. Nevertheless however justified or not, the sense of stress resulting can be considerable. We often legitimate organizational demands because they fulfil expectations of our own. But if we have a very clear self-identity we will not undertake activities which we do not feel confident in assuming and we will certainly avoid taking on activities which cause us pain.

> Not being able to say 'no' is a way of punishing ourselves because it puts us into an evaluative relationship with our colleagues.

PERSONAL SATISFACTIONS FROM SCHOOL

Lifestyle and organizational style

Schools, like all organizations, exist in a time frame of their own and this time frame is always smaller than each of their members' own. Schools take up only a part of our day and the rest of our time is determined by other considerations. Few of us observe the same daily pattern at home that we do at work. In purely organizational terms one day will be much like another though the experience of them may be different. Monday's timetable looks like Friday's but we experience Monday and Friday quite differently.

Our personal lifestyle is unlikely to be much like our style at school but most teachers manage to accommodate with little difficulty although some, especially young teachers, may have problems. Many of us change our spirit and outlook with the seasons, the weather and our personal relations outside school and this may cause unwelcome tension. We have to find ways of dealing with this tension when it arises because both our personal and employment life may be spoilt.

Too many of us make the place of employment more important than our domestic life with the consequence that what happens at work affects us too forcefully. We become vulnerable to happenings at work and this makes us more sensitive at home. We must keep all our activities in life in balance so that overall one aspect enriches the others and they combine to give us emotional support.

> Sadly, for some people, work is a substitute for other forms of living and they become unbearably burdened by how they fare at work. Remember the adage, Work to live not live to work.

The key to coping with schools is to believe that they are there to serve us not the other way round. The longer we stay in a school the more space we make for ourselves and the more room for manoeuvre. We can make it happen the other way round and build more and more restraints around us by taking on more and more duties. Schools can be strangely undemanding when everything is going well — and cruelly demanding when we are in trouble.

The better we understand how schools function as organizations the better will we find our way round to our own advantage. For one thing, no one is indispensable to school organization yet sometimes we behave as if we are; taking a day off for sickness becomes almost impossible for some people. Being indispensable is a consequence of our wishing to be, no one else makes us so.

> The real skill lies in making other people think you are indispensable while knowing that you are not.

In this way we can make the school serve our needs without harming anyone else.

Retaining personal integrity

It is esential always to maintain our personal integrity within the school. Schools can be quite demanding of personal loyaties in ways that go beyond the functional needs of the organization. Teachers are expected to be examples of social propriety outside the school and to exhibit a consistency of values both in the school and outside it. They may be in danger of sacrificing themselves to the impersonal; the school becomes a dominating idea but it is still an object not a person.

If, in the rhetoric of education, schools are about students finding and fulfilling themselves then they should do the same for teachers. Yet sometimes teachers exploit the students in their effort to find personal fulfilment. Personal integrity is achieved by being clear about what you want for yourself and being determined to get it but without anyone else having to suffer and preferably with collateral benefits for others.

> If we can be clear about the distinction between 'self' and 'other' we are not likely to do anyone else any harm.

The private life of the individual is precious. School and home must be sufficiently separate for us to have a full existence in both. The quality of the one will enrich the quality of the other but neither should be an extension of the other. This raises problems for students and the work they are expected to do at home.

There seems to be a set of unclarified assumptions about the relationship of the school to the home that parents do little to help with. Some students are glad to get to school because they are happier there, but some find that they have to take the unhappiness of school home with them in their homework. Is homework an unalloyed good thing?

The same considerations apply for teachers. Some find school more satisfying than home and others find it an imposition to have to take work home at night and at weekends. Where did the idea come from that teachers 'ought' to spend time away from school doing preparation? We need a richness in relationships at school and away from it. We need people who understand us and to whom we can talk in some depth. For most of us just being able to talk to someone is enough; if they will listen we can talk our problems through without the help of an expert.

COPING WITH MOODS

Moods and depression

Sometimes there are periods when the effort of helping ourselves proves just too much. Even the finding of someone to talk to is difficult to undertake. People who suffer severe depression get like this. They even find it difficult to admit that they are depressed. But fortunately however depressed we become there are fluctuations in our moods and moments of brightness when a little stimulus comes to do something about it. These moments have to be seized (they always can be). There are a number of causes; the commonest is the changes in our diurnal rhythms that lead to periods of greater cheerfulness and self-awareness. But once we have brought ourselves out of the darkness we will be greatly supported if there is someone else we can go to and share our feelings with.

Coping mechanisms

We all have moods of one sort or another and of varying intensity. But not all moods are depressive; we may feel lacking in energy but not depressed. We may also feel full of energy or overactive.

> The best way of dealing with moods and feelings is first to accept them and then respond positively — enjoy them, use them, even when they are uncomfortable.

When we find ourselves in a bad mood we can just accept it for what it is because acceptance is the first step towards coping with it. When we have an energetic mood, even if it comes at an inopportune time, we can accept it as the incitement to doing something purposeful and satisfying rather than frittering it away.

If often helps to share a mood with other people; invariably they will respond supportively even if they do not at that moment share it. Usually, it helps to share feelings about your work with colleagues. If you are not looking forward to taking a certain class it helps to talk to a friend about it because that begins to put things into perspective.

It has been said that nothing is so bad as you imagine it will be. This may be so most of the time but it is not true all of the time. There are occasions when events turn out worse than you anticipated. The best way to deal with such situations is to recall that by the time you have become aware of how bad the situation is it is part way over. Furthermore, the worse it gets the more you will have to talk about afterwards. In any case, if it is really bad it means other similar occasions won't seem so bad.

> The secret of dealing with the terrible is to take it as it comes and not to worry about how bad you feel about feeling bad.

One difficulty in being a member of a school is that there is a temptation to blame the school when things go wrong; it is the school that you feel is getting on top of you. But it cannot be the school, only some people in it and you will almost certainly be able to find others who sympathize with you and can share your experience and give support. The secret is to identify those people who cause you trouble and deal with them; don't lump everyone together as is so easily done.

It is not any individual so much as your reaction to them that causes the trouble, or the way you appraise them as part of your life experience. Only in the very rarest of cases does everyone feel equally turned off by the same person. When that person is the boss it will generally be because they are a convenient 'Aunt Sally' or scapegoat rather than that they are like that to their closest friends and families. When Harry Gray gets up your nose it is you who are allowing him to do so.

Subassertiveness

The problem is that most of us put ourselves at the mercy of 'the organization' rather than taking the organization on as something that can be made to work for us. To do this we have to be prepared to accept more responsibility for our part in the school. This form of dependency is sometimes called *subassertiveness*; it is when we have the expectation of others that they will do things for us without us having to do them for ourselves. Subassertiveness always leads to feelings of resentment since one feels put upon. It means we become lazy in looking after our own long-term interests.

If we want to be able to cope with school organization we must increase our independence from it and take on more personal responsibility. This is very difficult and cannot happen all at once, but you can make a start by reminding yourself that what you do has more to do with your choices than anyone else's. Even when you cannot change what you do, you have some influence over how you do it. You can also always change the way you look at anything you are asked to do.

Personal and shared feelings

One of the difficulties we have about our feelings is that we cannot know how others experience the same thing. Just because we find a colleague brash and self-centred it does not follow that other colleagues will experience them in the same way. Even if they use the same terms that we use they may not understand them in the same way. This is sometimes the problem in dealing with a head teacher. There seems to be general agreement that they are authoritarian and dominating, but no two people seem able to agree on a common instance of such behaviour in order to face them with their behaviour!

Conversation in the staff room can be quite rebellious and there may be loud declarations of revolt, but as soon as someone tries to organize a formal complaint all the support falls away because everyone has an excuse for not considering a common and specific action to be sufficiently offensive.

The problem has to do with subjective and objective experience. My experience and interpretation are never quite the same as anyone else's and so there is always a personal element in anything done or said even though it is apparently the same as someone else's. There is really very little school behaviour that can be said to be objective because it is always interpreted by individuals.

Sometimes there is not the reciprocity of feeling that we would like. It does not follow that if I dislike someone they dislike me or vice versa. We are not always good evaluators of ourselves, certainly not with regard to other people's views of us. But as we come to understand our own feelings and where they come from we are moving towards an 'objectivity' about ourselves. The better we understand something the more objective we are about it. Part of this understanding is not to attribute to others what we believe for ourselves without some substantiation. Many of us make untested assumptions about people we are not particularly close to in organizations and then are puzzled when on closer acquaintance we find they are not as we held them to be.

TECHNIQUES FOR MANAGING
OUR EMOTIONAL WELL-BEING

Taking time to relax

Without planned breaks the demands of work increase. Most teachers claim that it takes them several days of the school holidays (and in the summer sometimes several weeks) before they begin to relax. It may be that one of the problems for teachers in the day-to-day experience of the job is that few tasks are complete so there is a general level of dissatisfaction.

It is well-worth considering the extent to which a high dedication to the school is an excuse for not facing up to realities in our own life which are problematical. We can be unduly dedicated to the welfare of students in such a way that we actually impede their progress and their development to autonomy. On the whole schools try to control children too much and teachers sometimes takes an excessive responsibility.

Some teachers in the classroom may be engaging in an unhealthy self-indulgence. It is easy to wallow in being protective when it is really control that is the teacher's need. One difficulty of being responsible for others is that we have still to allow them their freedom. Freedom cannot be earned except by achieving independence and often this comes through disobedience. In any case, no teacher can carry the emotional burden of being fully responsible for a hundred or more children a day. No one could possibly know them well enough to begin to relate to them on a deep affective level. By protecting students teachers may well be protecting themselves; tight boundaries round the classroom become tight boundaries round the teacher.

> Teachers need to understand how they can stay in such good spirits that they do not misinterpret their role.

Health and coping

One of the obvious and fundamental ways of coping well with stress is in ensuring that we are fit and healthy. As we point out in Chapter 1, in our appraisal process, we take physical state into account and our health can influence our judgement. Families with babies are often stressed through lack of sleep over a period of time, and in the same way if you do not get enough sleep you can expect to find work potentially more difficult and stressful. Having a healthy lifestyle may sound boring but this does not mean an excess of sporting activity, for sporting activity can be just as stressful as anything else.

A healthy lifestyle is one where the balance for the individual is right among all those things that are of interest and concern. It involves doing things in fulfilling and varied ways. It involves relaxation and exercise, a full and rounded approach to life and its opportunities. At its core is peace of mind and contentment because that leads to appropriate choices of activity to engage in and the finding of inherent satisfactions in what you do.

Many teachers feel a sense of fatigue at the end of the day – and even during the day. It is a residual tiredness that we know is not a 'healthy' tiredness. It makes us just want to sit down and rest, and we do not feel attracted to going out or engaging in our usual interest.

Often the only way of combating *ennui* is to make yourself do something. Just get up and go out; go for a walk. Once you do this, your mood should change. You'll begin to enjoy what you're doing, and this leads you on to make yet more positive and active choices.

Once we allow ourselves to be tempted into indolence there is a downward spiral that requires more and more determination to reverse. It is like beginning to eat more when we gradually find our consumption of unnecessary food quickly escalates and we realize how much easier it is to put weight on than to take it off. The only way to combat these adverse changes is to introduce a little regular exercise into your life. Walk to the post-box each evening with a letter; meet someone on foot rather than collect them in the car; go out to buy the daily newspaper instead of having it delivered; pull up some weeds every time you go into the garden and so on.

Strategies for self-help

There are several ways of furthering our strategies for self-help. One way is through different levels of social involvement. We can think of coping strategies that are private or personal, those that are interpersonal, and those that are related to the ways an organization functions.

In Chapter 1 we explain the importance of the appraisal process and those factors which influence the way in which we might define ourselves as feeling stressed or not. Sometimes the difference between merely surviving and coping well is very little, and may be only be an expectation based on our faulty perceptions.

Knowing yourself and knowing your vulnerabilities enable you to do something positive about them.

If we know that as teachers we are prone to irritability when feeling slightly hungry we can ensure that we keep our blood-sugar level more constant either by eating the right foods or by a topping-up process. We are responsible for our problems and must acknowledge them if we are to deal with them. If, for example, we blame the school's timetabling for our irritability when the cause is our bad eating habits we will never come to deal with the problem.

Relaxation strategies

Individual ways of coping with stress are through dealing with our emotions and physical reactions to stress as well as more conscious ploys of compartmentalization, setting realistic goals and acknowledging our own success. We shall deal with emotional control first.

Since stress is a cognitive phenomenon, we can decide consciously to alter our physical condition to improve how we feel. This can be done on two levels.

First, practise relaxation and related techniques regularly. This is to prepare yourself physically for times of stress. Daily relaxation of some sort is important, as is daily exercise, to energize you. We all need a quiet time to ourselves to reflect on life. Some people do this by taking a sauna, others might sit quietly looking at the garden, others might stroke the cat; it is all a matter of personal preference.

The second level is to use relaxation techniques deliberately to calm down when you are actually stressed. This will be much more difficult to achieve if you are not well-practised in any form of relaxation. An example of this comes from the classes run for pregnant women who practise those exercises they will be called upon to use in childbirth.

The underlying assumption is that behaviours need to be 'overlearned' to reach mastery level and become automatic in order to be ready at times of stress. If strategies are not overlearned they tend to be forgotten in moments of great stress and previously learned but unhelpful strategies emerge. That is why many of us revert to apparently child-like behaviour when seriously stressed. We bring into use strategies which were overlearned as children and which have not been superseded by new, more mature ones. Tantrums are an example of this sort of problem; many adults do in fact have tantrums though in a disguised form.

> Relaxation strategies alone will not solve your problems. They may become ostrich-like behaviours which actually prevent you from solving problems.

But they can contribute to an overall feeling of well-being and save you from physiological ravages. We know that remarkable control of physical processes can be achieved. People can learn to control their heart beat; they can control their digestive juices to prevent ulcers forming; they can learn to control their brain-wave patterns and can even learn to prevent an epileptic seizure. All these skills take time to learn and are usually taught in exceptional circumstances but we can all learn a greater degree of control over our bodily functions.

There are many books about relaxation techniques so there is no need to go into detail here; we shall merely mention some techniques that prove generally useful. Readily at hand are such relaxation aids as hot baths and saunas which relax the muscles and give a feeling of warmth and comfort. There is also self-hypnosis, stress inoculation and desensitization.

Hypnosis

Hypnosis is widely misunderstood; people think of one individual falling under the evil control of another − as Trilby is controlled by Svengali in Du Maurier's novel. In fact, no one can be hyponotized against their will or made to do anything whilst in a trance that would normally be un-acceptable to them. You retain your personal integrity and also your privacy.

Hypnosis is probably best understood as a changed state of awareness which accompanies deep physical relaxation. The experience is very pleasant and enables the mind to concentrate on whatever the person chooses, without having to take any notice of what the body is doing. Often the technique of guided imagery is used to promote problem-solving. For example, if you consider your problem to be that you are fat, under hypnosis you can imagine yourself to be slim and also imagine doing things that you will not do in real life − like eating sensibly, not overindulging, eating only at meal times. In this way you can strengthen your resolve when not under hypnosis.

Self-hypnosis refers to the process of doing this for yourself without someone to 'hypnotize' you. There are plenty of audio tapes available to help in this. The process of learning will depend on how far you trust yourself. For many people it is another skill to be learned although some appear to be good at it quite naturally. Self-hypnosis can be learned as a method of inducing deep relaxation and for using imaging for problem-solving.

An example of ways of sorting out problems through imaging is to see your life to date as a desk with many drawers that need sorting out. The task is to throw out everything that is no longer useful or valued and to keep only things that accord with current events. This includes feelings about relationships with others, leftover feelings from childhood, the lack of acknowledgement from those people who are important for us. Aspects of our life can be tied up in a bundle to be discarded forever. This exercise is best done with someone to help you but when done under self-hypnosis can help you in ways not at all possible in ordinary consciousness.

Desensitization

Hypnosis can also be used to shorten or intensify processes involved in desensitization or stress inoculation. For example, in a desensitization programme the stages can be experienced under hypnosis and the effects be as great, in one or two sessions, as ten or more without hypnosis. Desensitization is a process only necessary in certain well-defined circumstances, and these may not occur very often in schools – except that they may do so more often for students than for staff. However, guidelines may help in recognizing the build-up to a problem so you can start to take action earlier; it may also offer an additional strategy for tackling some problems.

Desensitization is usually used when a person has developed a very strong but unreasonable fear in relationship to something or someone; it is usually called a *phobia*. The procedure assumes that in avoiding the feared thing (e.g. dogs) the person feels better but the avoidance itself leads to reinforced fear. We all experience something of this when we have doubts about something we used to be able to do easily. This is why when people are involved in an accident in a car or plane or whatever they go straight back and travel again; if they do not, their fear increases. The problem is that it is normal and healthy to avoid things that we fear or find uncomfortable and we only need to be cured of those fears that are unreasonable.

Dealing with phobias

In a sense, some teaching experiences are analogous. For example, fear of fifth formers may be increased by an avoidance of teaching them. What are the processes in desensitization? For the phobic person, attributes of the dreaded object or situation are isolated which contribute to their fear-provoking nature, and these are then placed in a hierarchy relating to how much anxiety is associated.

The intention is to keep the fear always within manageable limits so that the person can feel able to cope and feels successful in not panicking. In this way people learn to stop avoiding objects or the like that have taken on an almost magical quality. The process can be very successful in enabling people to live normal lives after living the limiting life of a phobic. Most people at some time or another develop unreasonable fears but all of us can conquer them. Someone who has an unreasonable fear is not 'mad' but has just fallen into a spiral of increasing fear.

There are many situations which may make us feel fearful and which we may try to avoid. If we combine relaxation with rehearsal — which is what desensitization is virtually all about — we can ensure that these fears do not get out of hand.

Stress inoculation

In many ways stress-inoculation training is similar to desensitization. The major difference is in the emphasis given in stress inoculation to monitoring self-statements. We have already mentioned the way that self-statements can influence the experience of stress by changing our appraisal of the situation. The idea is to substitute self-statements which will enhance effective coping and positive self-evaluation for those which will increase anxiety and self-doubt.

To begin with the individual has to learn to interpret the situation in a more helpful way by being encouraged to see the reaction to stress as a series of steps rather than as a massive, panic reaction. There are three steps in this stage: preparing for, confronting and handling a stressor; coping with the feelings of being overwhelmed; and making positive, reinforcing self-statements. Once you are able to do this, you can learn how to relax and to direct action to move either towards the stressor or away from it, according to which is the more appropriate. The third stage is most important and incorporates the overlearning of the new skills within a hierarchy of stressful events (as in the desensitization process).

Managing stress by managing goals

Other ways of personal coping are to do with how you set goals and evaluate your successes as well as compartmentalization. One of the factors that we all tend to take for granted (except in unusual circumstances such as being told we have only a short time left to live) is time. Time is very much a matter of our imagination and is coloured by our experience of it. We make priorities for ourselves that concern the use of time but they are themselves not about time but about preferences and choices, that is, about personal goals.

If we complain that we are short of time to achieve a goal, it is because we have preferred to do something else. If we say there is not enough time we mean that we have to do something for which we do not have the resources.

Over time itself we have no control nor does it belong to us to do anything with. We may choose to do things that squeeze others out and we have to look carefully to our personal values to understand why we consider somethings we do to be wasteful while we neglect those we consider important. We need to look carefully at our choices and preferences for certain goals so that we are ordered enough in our life to accommodate those activities we need. Foresight has many rewards. Others judge how important things are to us by the way we allocate time to them.

Compartmentalization

Compartmentalization is an aid to coping. We all envy people who can switch off or from one thing to another without any qualms. Compartmentalization requires practice as does any other skill. If you find compartmentalization difficult, ask yourself, Why cannot I separate one task from intruding on another? Sometimes compartmentalization is forced upon us when we are made to engage in another activity by friends or family though we do not feel in the mood for it. Such pressure helps to 'take us out of ourselves' and life becomes a little easier.

One advantage of compartmentalization is that is enables us to put our various jobs and interests into perspective so preventing them from running into one another. A row at work with a colleague feels different and less important when we get back home to family or friends.

Listening and talking

Most teachers rely on their personality and professional skills for coping in the classroom where they are for the most part on their own. They may also rely on their colleagues for help and assistance. We all need other people for help and it is an unnecessary presumption to think we can go it alone.

The advantage of consulting colleagues is that they understand our problems better than outsiders so far as getting matters into perspective from an internal point of view. A neighbour, however sympathetic, cannot know the finer and practical points of school life and cannot help us with factual or prescriptive advice however warm and sympathetic a listener they may be.

The basis of all help is listening. Just as someone can be supported by being listened to, so can listening to other people be supportive. There are very few occasions when someone else's problems or circumstances when related to us do not shed some light on our own condition. Being ready to listen may be a way of dealing with our own problems, because things fall into perspective when a colleague simply has to talk to us, and instead of us talking to them we become the listener. To do so we have had to weigh the importance of our need against the importance of the other person's and that is the start of solving our own problem.

> The essential quality of listening is that it is uncritical yet empathetic; the listener has high regard for the talker whatever the nature of the conversation.

The great advantage of talking is that it helps you to get your ideas straight. Even when we talk to ourselves it helps a little, but we are inclined to believe our own arguments so we need someone else to talk to.

> Thoughts that seemed very complex and matters which had assumed sinister significance often fall out to be trivial and not at all fearsome once you have tried to put them into words. Simply talking about a problem can solve it.

Talking about ideas can be an effective way of getting into touch with our feelings particularly if there is a sensitive listener who asks questions to clarify their − and, more important, our − understanding not to question our truthfulness.

Talking with someone else can also help to bring them into your reality, your world as you see it. Many teachers do not use their colleagues for this purpose but use other people who have no knowledge of the school as a work place. Outsiders have to try to understand how the teacher perceives life at school and if they listen carefully they can help in the clarification of perceptions. But there is some danger that they may interpose their own inapplicable memories on what the teacher says and further distort it.

> When we are really upset, the outsider is often a good person to turn to for putting things into a sensible relationship. Often the outsider sees matters to be the trivial things they are and can help us admit that without loss of face among colleagues.

Related forms of help are the giving of emotional support and emotional challenge. Though we all need emotional support we may not all realize that we need it. Some people know they need it but cannot ask for it in case it is refused, in which case they will feel hurt. Usually the people who need it most find it most difficult to ask for it or acknowledge it when it is given. It is a good rule of thumb to assume that it is always needed and even when rebuffed continue to offer it in a more ritualistic and impersonal way — general politeness and courteous behaviour.

We can also make sure that most of our behaviour towards others is confirming and supporting rather than critical and judgemental. If we ourselves need affirmation the surest way to receive it is by giving it.

> The best way of receiving feelings that we need is by showing them towards others because someone will always reciprocate sufficiently for our needs.

Emotional challenge is also something we need if we are to build up a robust emotional constitution. We need others to provide feedback about how they perceive our emotional responses and conditions if we are to be able to use them effectively.

A similar aspect of social support which divides into support and challenge is the support which is technical and relates to our professional skills. We need appreciation of the work we do but we may need to ask for this. Likewise we need feedback about our skills and if it is not forthcoming voluntarily we must ask, since unless we have a realistic assessment of our job performance we can be easily caught off balance in a crisis.

We also need to be realistic about organizational demands and to make sure that no one else creates our job for us. Talking to colleagues from other schools is a way of understanding whether our job really contains all the elements we put into it. We should always make certain we keep the school organization at a safe distance and not allow it to take possession of us.

7
HELPING OTHERS (1): STUDENTS

● Coping with responsibility ● Facilitation eases stress ● Personality hang ups in the classroom ● Supporting student needs ● Dealing with conflict crises ● Systematizing student care

COPING WITH RESPONSIBILITY

Teaching is not traditionally considered to be one of the 'helping professions' though it does involve a great deal of helping and caring, particularly in the early years of infant and primary schooling and in the provision for special educational needs.

One of the difficulties in defining the relationship between teacher and student is that so many ambiguities arise from the idea of 'in loco parentis' by which many teachers believe themselves bound. Since there is no commonly held view of what a good parent would do in any general circumstance (and often in any given instance) there is plenty of room for teachers to exercise personal judgement. Indeed, for any class of students the variation in what parents want for their children will be considerable and in many cases, especially the controversial ones, the variations will contain contradictions.

It seems an unusual hardship for teachers to be held responsible for knowing the wish of parents when so many different wishes are involved.

Responsibility to students

A sensible teacher will reject any idea of being able to guess what all (or even any) parents might want for their children and will concentrate on doing what seems best in terms of his or her own values. In a way, trying to guess what other people would want is a way of avoiding responsibility not accepting it. It is also a way of trying to coerce colleagues particularly in its public expression when 'what parents really want' is used as an argument for a point of view, often a conservative one.

A teacher who is concerned with the general welfare of his or her students will adopt a common sense attitude of helpfulness and will accept that students need a lot of emotional support in their studies and that a teacher's job requires that student needs have priority for attention. The great danger in working with people younger than ourselves is that we may project some of our unresolved needs and problems onto them. To achieve a good relationship with one and all we must respect their dignity and allow them the same rights and privileges that we assume for ourselves; teachers sometimes forget that students have these rights too.

In many ways the organization of schools does not recognize that students have rights in the same way as adults have with the consequence that teachers assume more of a custodial role than a parental one; a corrective role rather than a helping one.

Discipline and stress

It is quite clear that a lot of teacher stress arises from the policing aspects of the teaching role; the custodial and repressive actions that managing schools involves, especially secondary schools. Teachers may feel that repression and undue control are required of them even in a benign regime, a demand that comes as much from the head as the reactive behaviour of students.

Many teachers see students as essentially hostile, potentially likely to get out of hand, and as a threat to good order unless rigorously directed. Many teachers fear losing control of their classes more than anything else and evaluate one another on class control as a primary dimension. The fear of losing control arises from a sense of separation from the students, a sense that order and control can only be imposed and cannot arise out of a collaboration among the interested parties.

It is a strange perspective on any class of students to expect hostility as inevitable rather than to assume that collaboration would be acceptable as the best mode of working together. But the more a teacher takes responsibility on behalf of the students the less responsive will be the students to regulating their own behaviour. Domination and authoritarianism on the part of the teacher are educationally self-defeating since they do not require anything other than acquiescence from the students while the teacher is with them.

> The more a teacher dominates the more alienated will the students be in consequence and the greater likelihood there is of rebellion.

The basic requirement for good order (or discipline) in the classroom is that those involved should understand that it is in their mutual interest to maintain it. For everyone there should be rewards. Punishments are, of course, a negation of rewards and at their best have a very short effective life; they have to be continually reinforced.

The giving of punishments originates in the mind of the punisher and underlines their need for control of the punishment and the punished. Evaluation, however, originates in the mind of the receivers and the actions of others are considered pleasurable or otherwise in the receiver's terms.

> Young teachers often fail to understand that discipline is a characteristic of the whole class — themselves included — rather than a condition imposed by a single individual.

The mistake teachers make is either to offer no rewards to the students or to offer inducements that are surplus to the occasion. Once the balance has been achieved the matter of discipline is self-regulating and becomes one of the more important aspects of a helping relationship.

Discipline in the classroom is a consequence of the willingness of all parties to co-operate in the performance of agreed and acceptable activities. Self-discipline is a consequence of an individual taking charge of their own learning. The task of the teacher is to gain the co-operation of students in doing something that is meaningful to them.

> There are two ground rules for the creation of a good working atmosphere in the classroom: one is to ensure that students want to do what they are asked to do, and the other is to help them to be able to do it.

Success is achieved by negotiation between two 'equal' partners in the decision. Experienced teachers know that unless students feel they have made the best choice for themselves they will not co-operate.

Schools where the climate is a consequence of teachers' wishing to dominate and be authoritarian make life very difficult for teachers whose values are not of this kind. Students may rebel against the non-authoritarian teachers in compensation for their treatment by the bossy ones. Inexperienced teachers may suffer very badly in such a school and may be puzzled as to why they did not have problems before, without realizing that their previous experience was in a more benign environment.

Even experienced teachers who are not by nature authoritarian will have problems, one of which is having to ease up on the demands they make on students while they unwind from overdisciplined classes. They have to provide time and space to absorb the frustrated animosities that are directed against the authoritarian teachers.

Furthermore, authoritarian teachers encourage students to perceive non-authoritarian teachers as lax and soft. Accepting authoritarianism is an easy way of shelving personal responsibility, and authoritarian norms can be quite tenacious. However, the opposite sometimes happens in that in a collaborative school authoritarian teachers will have problems of order and discipline because the norms are reversed; students will just not be impressed by a dominating approach and may rebel effectively against a hard classroom regime. In the long run, when students rebel authoritarian teachers are more likely to suffer stress than collaborative teachers simply because they do not have the repertoire of approaches to draw on and their appraisal of the situation is more personally threatening.

There is a good deal of irrationality in the thought that without firm control children will go rushing all over the place in a state of disorder and general destructiveness. One of the difficulties is in the definition of *firmness* which varies from being supportive to being dictatorial. It is reasonable to assume that everyone benefits from support but this is not the issue.

> Human behaviour is always purposeful even it is sometimes misguided and ineffective.

Behaviour is always a response to something; it doesn't just happen spontaneously. Therefore classroom behaviour is always a response to something that has happened in the classroom and it relates directly to its causes. So if a teacher does not like what the students are doing he or she needs to find out why it is happening and negotiate a change. Fortunately people are reasonable and will always respond to an opportunity to talk about what they are doing.

It may be that the teacher is directly responsible for the undesirable behaviour; in fact the likelihood is that that will be so.

> Unless a teacher is prepared to consider that they may be the cause of class problems there can be no real dialogue. The cause of most continuing discipline problems is lack of dialogue.

Breakdowns in relationships and poor student behaviour in schools are always a consequence of long-standing problems and can never be solved by crude simplistic measures. Invariably the necessary condition for improvement will be a change in attitudes towards the students rather than the other way round.

FACILITATION EASES STRESS

Teachers as facilitators

The term *facilitator* is creeping into use in teaching following the developments in new programmes where the students 'negotiate' in some way the work they do, how they do it and how the evaluation will take place. The argument is that if students feel that they have decided what they want to learn they will be more committed to what they do and will be more able to ask for help when they need it. Instead of the teachers making all the decisions they help the students to make decisions for themselves and they adopt a helping role with this purpose as central.

It marks a significant shift from the days when teachers made all the decisions and expected the students to follow them. Instead of 'selling' what the subject is about, teachers have to work with the students to find some agreement on what the student considers meaningful; they then have to help them to follow up their decisions without taking responsibility away from them. Many teachers do not like the idea of this kind of partnership in learning and are unwilling to support it, but schools have changed from places where students could be expected to do what teachers decided to places where they demand a closer involvement.

Facilitation places teachers in a helping relationship in which they have to help students to identify learning needs and help them to plan a course of action to supply them. In its more extreme forms − such as MSC training programmes − the students simply will not respond unless there is adequate negotiation and teachers have little option but to accommodate them. In schools the idea that teachers know best may still be dysfunctionally strong.

> The concept of teacher as facilitator means that the teacher is concerned with the function of assisting with the process of learning rather than simply the determination of content.

There is an enormously long tradition, especially in further education, of the teacher as 'instructor' whose job is to ensure that the student (apprentice or trainee) can perform certain practical and technical functions. It also assumes that those skills were pretty well defined and exact. The instructor tradition is very strong in education but is not properly 'education' because it neglects so many aspects of learning that cannot be reduced to physical skills.

In infant teaching it leads simply to 'barking at print' − that is, being able to pronounce the sounds without understanding the meaning of the words. In technician training it means being able to use a screwdriver but not being able to discriminate when alternative means of adhesion are desirable. A good deal of 'programmed' learning lacks the conceptual and discriminatory aspects of personal learning because its mechanical analysis leaves out the individuality of personal learning styles. Cramming is the most traditional manifestation; it might get you through the examination but you forget it all afterwards. Furthermore, instruction implies that learning pursues a relentless purpose largely of its own and irrespective of the learner. Driving instruction is a case in point. One takes a course of driving lessons with the sole objective of passing the test but many people do not truly learn to drive until they have passed the test.

Education is not something that can be packaged in the way of driving tests but is an ongoing process, always unfinished and open-ended, continually leading from one thing to another and forever catching the attention and interest of the learner drawing them into new fields and fresh experiences.

> Education is, above all, about the development of the whole person, not the acquiring of technical skills in a disembodied form.

Education and training

One of the long-standing arguments about *education* and *training* has been whether training is little more than instruction while education is concerned with the whole person. Many industrial trainers would say that education (in the fuller sense) is an essential part of training and that considerable attention is given to personal development on industrially and commercially based courses. There seems to be no real debate about the two terms being substantially different in practice, though training may be more vocationally orientated for reasons of its provenance in industry.

Teachers may feel themselves stressed just because they are uncertain of the relationship of education to training. Without a training element education for most students is meaningless and perhaps too much school 'education' comes over as purposeless and without relevance or apparent usefulness in life situations because teachers are often too vague about what they are doing. A form of schooling which is all about the finer things in life without an anchoring in basic matters cannot have much meaning to a learner who is trying to make sense of the practicalities of life. If education becomes rarified it cannot provide the oxygen needed for life support.

PERSONALITY HANG UPS IN THE CLASSROOM

Elements of personal relationships

Whenever we come into personal contact with other people we draw on our own personal qualities, dispositions, strengths, weaknesses, attitudes, prejudices, experience. A short-tempered teacher is a short-tempered person. How we behave in the classroom is a direct manifestation of how we behave in any circumstances we perceive as similar.

But there are various important ways we play out our weaknesses in any relationship, as well as our strengths. We bring our 'hang ups' into our relationships ready to be exploited at the appropriate cue. Our hang ups interfere with our relationships whatever the stance we take towards other people but when we are in an authoritarian relationship the consequences can be very serious because our 'subordinates' are less able to provide feedback on our behaviour; and, of course, they have no option over obeying us.

For example, teachers with a personal hang up or obsession about cleanliness may project this onto their pupils and become obsessed with neatness and tidiness in such a way as to cause great concern to the student. Not infrequently, teachers use a class as a captive and unprotesting audience for the exploitation of ideas unresolved in their own minds. For another example, a preoccupation with sex and sexuality may lead to excessive references to sex in class. On the other hand, topics of unresolved concern may well lead to an enrichment of teaching. Teachers who have themselves been troubled sexually may feel able to help their students in their learning in an area much imbued with emotion.

The classroom is not the proper place for sorting out the teacher's own personal difficulties. However, most normal adults have areas of unresolved problem, and it is inevitable that many teachers should in some way or another use their students to work out their own emotional problems even though this will be done indirectly for the most part. Because students tend to be less mature than colleagues, there is a danger that personal problems remain unresolved and suddenly become critical in unexpected ways.

In the more socially (and politically) controversial areas the teacher will be in a 'no win' situation. When parents complain, their reaction can cause surprise and distress because teachers are often naïve enough to think that parents have almost limitless tolerance and share a teacher's common sense, progressive stance. Not so.

> Among parents will be represented every extreme of both tolerance and bigotry. The most vocal will be nearer the extremes than the centre.

Teachers have to learn to tread the middle way while alerting their students to major areas of controversy. This means that teachers must be very well-informed on the topics they choose to introduce and able to act as moderator and referee while their students take sides. There is a danger that a teacher might take advantage of a position of authority and not realize the extent to which they are stifling debate rather than encouraging it.

Perhaps a good deal of teacher disappointment arises from the failure of students to respond to a teacher's interests which are believed to be fairly put but which are little more than an expression of personal opinion with which the students feel no need to agree. It would be wrong to assume that teachers are interested in a rapport based only on their teaching subject and not at all on other interests and emotional responses. Teachers all have favourite students and they need to understand why. Some of the biggest disappointments come from favourite pupils and some of the greatest emotional traumas come from unrequited affection.

The strain of organized learning

For most — perhaps all — students, learning is a strain. For one thing, what and how they learn is regulated by the teacher and in the traditional classroom they have less control than in a progressive one over what and how they learn. Very few of us are able to learn fully in the pattern determined by someone else, however skilled a teacher we may have. Yet school students are continually subject to someone else's demands and ways of working. Content-led curricula lead to overstructuring and over-pressuring while learner-led curricula (though more open to student regulation) are still not free from the pressures of organizational demands.

Few adults could cope with the learning demands of the secondary-school day; indeed many teachers find it difficult. The relentless pressure of work — listening, responding, writing, reading, completing work, etc. — bears down upon students day by day, reinforced by the pattern of the term. No wonder everyone is ready for a holiday at the end of the term, for three times a year a marathon is run from which no one can be excused.

Teachers themselves seem largely unaware how much pressure they put themselves under to get through the syllabus and to cajole their students to keep pace with them. Whenever a teacher sets an assignment it has to be 'marked' and the more set the more there are to mark. All these work pressures are induced by the teacher not the students and arise from the teacher's own sense of responsibility which may be outrageously wrong.

Often teachers try to prove things for themselves but use their students to do so. Students find ways of avoiding some of the teacher-imposed excesses but the teachers do not; some classes are a lesson in self-punishment for the teacher not hard work for the students, especially when the preparation time is included. One of the more bizarre forms of self-punishment is keeping students behind after school because the teacher must be the last to leave and is thus punished most.

Students suffer a good deal overall at the hands of their teachers. Not only may they be overworked but they have to put up with the idiosyncrasies of their teachers who are no less eccentric than the population at large. For some students being forced to go to school at all is punishment but when to this imprisonment is added a series of indignities — being made to sit in silence, being forbidden to go to the lavatory, having to play sports whether they like it or not, being set passages to learn by heart, etc. — then going to school is an unwelcome imposition. It is no excuse to say that the discipline of school will do them good; perhaps it will.

The point is that for students at the time they experience it, if being in school is stressful then that is what it is. Teachers are prone to overlook that for many students many aspects of school are unpleasant and they tolerate it often as the easiest way of coping with it not because it fills their days with delight.

SUPPORTING STUDENT NEEDS

Teachers tend to reinforce the bad aspects of school rather than the good ones, perhaps because they think that 'being soft' will be bad for the students. The point is not that 'happiness' should be a permanent condition for school but that most of us respond better when happy than when not, and few people would justify schooling if it were generally believed to create a great deal of unhappiness.

Traditionally, teachers have taken scant notice of student needs except when they are associated with extreme forms of disability, e.g. deafness, blindness, physical disability, etc. or as an excuse for low achievement. Only very recently have schools made provision for children with various handicaps because previously many were segregated in special provision. A consequence is that schools show most interest in the more able students and consider the somewhat less able as somehow not trying hard enough or not suitably placed.

Schools often show a preference for intellectual pursuit and have largely ignored emotional needs. Teachers resent being thought of as nursemaids or childminders though they must be such if they are to create the conditions for learning. Many teachers are ill-equipped to deal with student needs at the affective level and are often awkward when they try.

When students cannot do their work because it is intellectually difficult, they need care and support at the affective level before they can take the next step; they need support, encouragement, confirmation and warmth to be able to overcome their sense of failure. If help is offered in a too challenging, mean way it is both ineffective and damaging. A teacher who is too cold and distant from the students will only succeed in increasing the coldness and distance, alienate the students and fail to achieve the personal satisfactions that would normally be inherent in the job.

The importance of pupil self-regard

It is probably true for all of us that we need love and affection in some form or another and the amount we normally receive falls short of what we need. Lots of adults cry out for 'love' in all sorts of ways yet most would be horrified if they were told that is what they were doing. We all ask for strokes — approval, support, acceptance, regard, congratulations, etc. With many adults this is where their childhood needs show strongly. Of course our needs are served differently for all of us and the more mature we are the less demanding we are that they should be publicly given. Sadly many schools choose to give rewards and praise to only a few of their students — the more 'successful' — and to withold confirming strokes from the majority.

It is a salutory exercise to check with our friends how they fared at school and we will soon see that some of our best friends were mediocre at school, were often in trouble, won no prizes, had quite undistinguished careers, and yet we have no difficulty whatsoever in relating well to them. Yet schools make highly selective judgements about students in the formative years of their lives. Given all the external pressures on schools to perform these undesirable social functions, the only way the harm can be mitigated is if teachers have the right personal qualities, the chief of which in this respect is a high sense of personal regard.

The only sure basis for an accepting attitude to others is a proper, realistic and positive regard for yourself.

Parents with low self-esteem tend to project this onto their children, who develop the same low view of themselves.

Teachers need to feel good about themselves if they are to help their pupils to feel good.

The best way to help students to a high level of self-esteem is to create a learning process in the classroom which centres on them and their achievement and aims to show that they can all be achievers. Certain teaching approaches — such as learner-centred and discovery-based — do this better than others. The problem is that for the most part teachers are not trained to work in these ways and few schools are set up to facilitate it.

Teachers who try to introduce these approaches which are theoretically better than traditional formal methods are likely to experience some difficulty because of the contrast between the regime in their classroom and that in others. Unless teachers are very sure of what they are doing, they are better advised to deviate only a little (if at all) from the prevailing norms of the school. Experiment should normally be cautious, small and incremental.

It is foolish to put ourselves at risk for the sake of ideals when the nature of those ideals will not be appreciated. Teachers who put themselves at risk are harming students as well as themselves but are also making it difficult to bring about change when the situation becomes more auspicious. There is always a right time to bring about change and in a school context it must be done with adequate support from the head.

DEALING WITH CONFLICT CRISES

Origin of crises

Because classrooms are places of social interaction they are arenas for conflict of various kinds since even normal social relationships involve various levels of conflict of one kind or another. This means that teachers require a high level of skill in conflict resolution, arbitration and reconciliation. All organizations — and classrooms are organizations as much as schools are — are characterized by conflict, its suppression and, we hope, its resolution.

Most school crises are the result of the accumulation of a series of ultimately interlocking and accruing conflicts that have gone unacknowledged until they well up into an unmanageable crisis. Big crises are never unrelated to what has gone before, are never isolated events, but are the consequence of issues that have been allowed to pass unattended. Usually the incidents that spark off crises attract other issues that are tangential to them but which concern the same actors, and the task of dealing with them requires the various strands to be unravelled in the right order.

On the whole, teachers do not welcome feedback from their students about what happens in the classroom unless it be of a positive and approving kind. Teachers are generally unwilling to change their ways in response to students except in minor ways. Understandably, teachers have a personal style of teaching which they nurse against most criticism.

> Responding to student views in a positive way by full and open discussion of the method of teaching is the best way of dealing with many incipient problems.

Most students want to feel valued and appreciated so when teachers organize their classes in ways that treat individual students unfairly, they are preparing the ground for dissatisfaction and rebellion. The resolution of conflict situations proceeds best in small steps and each step deals with some small grouse or complaint. Schools may not be as good, as teachers often like to believe, at dealing with personal and interpersonal problems because they often transform them into administrative solutions – putting a student in another class or, in extreme cases suspending a student.

> The stress of being a class teacher often arises from not having adequate skills in conflict resolution so that all the energies that should go into teaching (that is, the fostering of learning) have to go into suppression or avoidance of conflict rather than its resolution.

Stress avoidance through co-operation

It is a truism that the best way of preventing stress in both students and teachers is by good management techniques in both the school and the classroom. Good management involves keeping individual interests in balance and will prevent many stress-inducing circumstances from arising; and when they do it will put the solving of the interpersonal and personal problems before the continuance of teaching.

At its simplest, good management leads to good order which is the basis on which adaptation occurs. Nothing is more upsetting in the classroom than unplanned disorder and unpredictability; students like to know where they are in their relationships both with teachers and their fellows. The introduction of novelty and fresh challenges is impossible without a sound base of order and emotional comfort, but the creation and support of good order is a joint responsibility for everyone in the group or class not just one person, the teacher.

Classroom management ought to be a shared task but it is often impeded by authoritarianism and autocracy. The security of familiarity becomes the stress of oppression if a teacher makes all the decisions unilaterally or manages every event without the co-operation of those involved.

> Teachers take too much upon themselves, forgetting that their students are as capable of making proper decisions about their learning as they are; if they are not, the lessons are pitched at the wrong level.
>
> Co-operation by its very nature leads to a mutuality of support while autocracy leads to alienation, individualism withdrawal and anomie.

Co-operation does not come about just by demanding it; it has to be developed through activity. On the whole, people prefer to work together co-operatively whatever they may sometimes say to the contrary. To start work with a class by assuming that lessons will not work by co-operation seems singularly perverse. There can be little doubt that teachers who take all the responsibility for classroom order to themselves are storing up a degree of potential stress that will in the long run prove disastrous — for them.

SYSTEMATIZING STUDENT CARE

Teaching and caring

Regardless of the age of the students, and sometimes regardless of the teaching tasks required, there are always teachers who take special interest in students' welfare and well-being. There are also in every school teachers who define their job in a narrower way and concentrate on a more pedagogic approach. Those teachers who have a strong sense of caring may seek jobs with special responsibility for pastoral work. Other teachers, in primary schools for example, may find they can incorporate their particular interest into their self-defined role as class teacher. In small schools, head teachers are also able to take on considerable pastoral care work, if they want to.

There are, then, two aspects to teachers enacting this sort of role — the will to do it and the way to do it. Not only do teachers have to have personal interest in the area to be successful but they also have to have the appropriate skills and information or knowledge. Many of us have been amazed at the types of problem some of our colleagues have been prepared to tackle when perhaps the more experienced among us (and more skilled!) would have sought help from another source, having recognized the problem as outside our range of competence.

Teachers and student wrongdoing

The biggest problem for students when teachers try to help them is that teachers tend to switch from one role to the next without warning. A good example of this is where a child may be suspected of committing a misdemeanour. The teacher says that if the child owns up all will be forgiven and the interview starts with calm and positive regard but slides into interrogation, proceeds through lecturing on morality and restitution and ends with some form of punishment being administered. This kind of betrayal of trust comes as a shock to students at first but more experienced students are wise to the wiles of their teachers and are not taken in.

Students sometimes own up to a misdemeanour just to get it over with or to expiate another offence even though they may be innocent. Particularly for younger students the morality of the teachers is not within their comprehension; they may well have a quite different sense of what is right and acceptable behaviour. Many school 'crimes' are institutional not matters of general morality. Teachers seem to believe, however, that under interrogation students tell the truth even though they might not believe them in other circumstances. It is the admission of guilt that is believed and rarely the admission of innocence – for the latter only prolongs the questioning.

Another problem is that students can be browbeaten by the more powerful role of teacher and they may just go along with teacher talk rather than engaging in true dialogue. The result of this failure – and the failure of the intervention strategy – is usually placed at the door of the pupil for not trying or breaking a contract or not caring. But this is not necessarily the case; it merely signals to the teacher that the student was not able to engage in a dialogue with them to solve the problem.

What is required is that the teacher works with the student to define the problem rather than the teacher defining the problem and imposing that definition on the student.

The student may not see the situation as problematic at all in which case negotiation will have to take place to solve the teacher's problem, which is consequently quite different.

There are better ways of going about an initial interview with a student and they must include giving the student the option of refusing the help offered. To be able to make a better choice the student must be informed of the range of ways in which the teacher can help, rather than being faced with a vague generalized promise to help.

Teachers have good intentions when they offer help to students but are frequently unreliable because they lack the patience to listen carefully and appropriately with the result that students become wary of them. When a contract has been negotiated about the nature of help offered and accepted, reliability is crucial on the part of the helper otherwise the student feels unimportant and not to be taken seriously.

Creating trust

Related to the notion of reliability is that of confidentiality. Students may assume that a teacher will keep their confidence or they may assume that others may be informed. That assumption is made independently of any assumption the teacher may make and for reasons only known to the student. A child who confides that he or she has been sexually abused almost certainly wants others to be told who are in a position to do something about it. But a student who discusses fears about his or her homosexuality may want this information to be kept strictly secret.

There are some situations when a teacher is legally obliged to inform others and it is as well to know what these are. At the beginning of any help being offered, the ground rules must be made clear so that the student understands the conditions under which you are obliged by law to inform others. In situations where it is unnecessary to inform others but would be helpful, the usefulness of telling others should be discussed with the student. The teacher is bound to seek permission first of all so that he or she may negotiate on the student's behalf. But the student must be the one who decides how much further anything they say goes.

> Some very damaging situations arise when students are of the opinion that there is strict confidentiality but discover that what they have said has been shared with other teachers. Sometimes they find this out only when they are shamed in front of their classmates by a teacher who was not party to the discussion.

All these matters are really commonsensical and would be taken account of more if they were between adults, but where children are involved teachers often appear to have a different moral code. Teachers can easily abandon the normal respect they would offer once they find themselves in difficulty with their students or dealing with matters which cause them some personal disquiet. This is especially true of sexual behaviour which teachers find very difficult to cope with in their students. Students come from a wider social circle than that in which a teacher will normally move and the standards, values and social norms may be offensive to the teacher; but this cannot be allowed to influence a teacher's attitude to a student.

A friendly, uncritical ear is supportive and helps the speaker to cope better. Sudden censoriousness can be devastating and must be avoided whatever the listener thinks. In a school setting, further and more specific help may be required, particularly if the student is concerned about confidentiality, reliability and accurate definition of the problem.

Outside help

The teacher needs to know how to obtain help from outside the school: who to turn to, where to go and how to ask for it. There is a wide range of 'hit and run' experts who can offer support and guidance to students both directly and indirectly through parents and teachers. But the least helpful thing to do is call in the expert and expect a magic wand to be waved forthwith. A number of problems arise from trying to pass responsibility for the student over to someone outside the school.

For instance, the pupil may be redefined as being outside the responsibility of the school either technically or figuratively; communication between the school and the expert may become attenuated; the school might defer to the expert instead of entering a dialogue; the problems may be seen as the student's only without reference to the share the school has in them; parental guilt might arise from a perceived escalation of the problem; parents may be confused about responsibility. Experts are powerful helpers only if they are used properly – that is, in a collaborative role to help define the problem and sustain a sensible interpretation of it.

The school must find the solution to its own problems and the responsibility cannot be transferred to an outside expert. A major contribution that visiting experts may make in relation to individual students is where the student is prepared to negotiate a problem definition and solution with the expert instead of with a teacher, if this is the only option the student is prepared to take. But it is an expensive waste of the expert's time to expect the outsider to be able to solve the contextual elements in the problem and assume responsibility for success once the student returns to the school.

Teacher stress and student stress related

There are many ways of helping students that involve also helping colleagues. As we constantly point out, no one acts in isolation and the stress experienced by a student may well be closely related to the stress felt by a teacher; and the other way round. In some ways it is strange that in schools it is only students who are selected for special help as an ongoing aspect of their education while teachers are never considered to be in need of help. It would be an indication of a healthier school where student and teacher stress were perceived as equal and related problems and to receive equally helpful intervention.

Perhaps, contrary to what may at first appear to be the case, it is the teachers who lose out by it not being recognized that they are under considerable stress. Teachers who are not helped to cope with their own stressful condition become a general menace to the students. The behaviour of a teacher under considerable stress may often pass for the acceptable 'eccentricity' or being a 'character' that fills the folklore of schools in the popular imagination.

Any help students receive will be of indirect help to teachers. Students can be given skills to reappraise the situations they find themselves in and to help them with their interpersonal relationships. One way to assist with appraisal is to provide information that enables a fuller view of a situation to be taken and which will increase insight as a consequence.

Counselling for self-appraisal

Counselling is one way to assist students to reappraise themselves and their situations. There are many guides to good practice in this area but teachers should identify a counselling style that suits them personally. A major requisite for successful counselling is time, especially reserved time, that is allowing a predetermined period long enough to be able to get into the problem the student wants to talk about. When time is reserved the counsellor agrees to devote the time to listening, something which is very rarely allowed in the normal school day. Counselling requires considerable training and practice of a very demanding kind and for many teachers requires attitudes and skills that they do not apply to their role as teachers.

Group work

Another way of enabling students to reappraise situations and themselves is by the use of small groups. These groups may be set up to draw together students with similar problems or may involve a mixture of students to enable them to benefit from each other's strengths and experiences. As in all ways of helping, ground rules need to be established for the duration of the exercise. Confidentiality is essential and sometimes secrecy concerning the existence of the groups may be required.

Running groups with students in the same school can be very difficult for teachers with little experience of group work, and to start with they should join another more experienced teacher or an expert in group work from outside, at least until the group is established. A wide range of activities and forms may be employed with such devices as role-playing, discussions, problem-solving, drama and co-counselling. The great advantage of working with groups is that students are often able to accept comments more readily from peers than from teachers. Such comments are often spontaneous rather than premeditated or stored up.

> Students with problems have often tried out a lot of strategies for coping and will have a wider experience than many teachers and can share them with other students.

Another useful aspect of group work is that targets for the week can be set which are negotiated publicly – as in slimmers' clubs – and so increase motivation and commitment.

Groups can also be invaluable in helping students to acquire and practise skills such as social-skills training where feedback from others is paramount. Social skills are important for those students who get into trouble at school through persistent misbehaviour. Often such students are poorer than their peers at identifying the non-verbal signals of teachers and in appreciating the subtler signals that teachers use to tell students they are becoming annoyed or angry. The student who continues to fool around in class when the rest have calmed down is probably just unaware of the teacher's signals rather than deliberately disruptive.

Student role models

Students may have poor social skills in terms of not being able to make friends and so they make immature approaches (e.g. 'Be my friend or I'll thump you'). It needs to be remembered that students may operate socially in a very different milieu from the school but be very successful there. Being socially competent relies not only on having skills but on using them appropriately. Some pupils lack the confidence to engage in appropriate social interactions, while others lack skills rather than confidence.

Some students have only poor models to copy; they may live in a family where the adults flare up quickly and have a shouting match; or where no one does anything until someone becomes angry. The student may only be aware of shouting and aggressive teachers at school and may respond to them as they do at home.

Social competence

Social-competence training is a somewhat neglected aspect of schooling and something of a side interest even when it is taken seriously. Apart from very young pupils and those with special educational needs, the development of social competencies is taken very much for granted. It is assumed to occur and be fostered without direct or overt teaching and only the hidden curriculum touches on issues of social skills. We are not referring here to what have come to be called competency in 'life skills' or 'survival skills' (e.g. boiling eggs, catching buses, applying for benefits). Here we mean the normal skills of social interaction in everyday life in ordinary situations but which are the prerequisite for living a full and rewarding life. This requires insight into other people's perspectives on life and seeing their needs as different from ours. It also means comprehension of social institutions and how they work, being able to interpret accurately social situations, make moral judgements and relate to others in ways that are personally satisfying.

Internalized behaviour

In any school curriculum some of these aspects will be pervasive but not overtly taught. Schools are institutions regulated from above and hence not societies congenial to the learning of social skills since standards of behaviour are imposed not negotiated, which is a condition of internalized behaviour. Furthermore, schools tend to take single option views of correct and incorrect behaviour and do not permit the variations and nuances that are current in normal life outside.

> If social skills were openly taught, students would be more questioning of rules and the authority of teachers would be more often opposed. But there would be infinitely better communication between teachers and students.

Schools need to develop a much more open and flexible attitude to student behaviour — in the way many further education colleges have done — if their students are to learn the kinds of social rather than conformist skills that will be required of them in the world outside.

An important way of helping students is in enabling changes to be made in personal relationships. This can be facilitated by any teacher in a variety of ways but firstly by negotiation. Much information about students is gained from staff-room talk and can also be changed by using this same mechanism. One teacher can change the perspective of other teachers by making positive comments about a pupil; expressing pleasure with progress and behaviour rather than joining in the general fault-finding.

Often a student's reputation is based upon flimsy and inaccurate evidence or shop talk, so changing the information base will help to redefine the picture teachers have of the student. If a student is experiencing particular difficulties, this approach can be used privately and quite deliberately with selected teachers. If this way does not work, it is possible to advise the student about how to influence the way a teacher responds. A simple example is encouraging a student to smile at the teacher on entering the classroom or to look positive when the teacher looks at them.

Sometimes a caring teacher can help students in practical ways to prepare for another teacher who presents them with problems – seeing that pens and rulers are ready, that they have the right textbooks, that preparation work has been completed, etc. What the teacher is doing in this case is rehearsing students in the ways that will help them to improve the quality of experience in class and so build up confidence to the point when they can take charge of themselves. This approach can be extended to self-monitoring.

Self-monitoring is when a student keeps a record of his or her own performance in particular areas and a parallel record is kept by teachers for comparison purposes and discussion with the student. The idea is to sensitize students to their own behaviour. Many people are unaware of what they do and sometimes shocked when they find out (for example, when seeing themselves on video). Once you have become aware of some undesirable habit you can prepare for it and prevent it happening by changing your behaviour slightly. Keeping records helps students to understand their own behaviour, makes them more likely to want to change it themselves, and so improve their behaviour.

A related area, though a controversial one, is behaviour modification. Although there have been undoubted abuses in the application of mechanistic approaches to changing people's behaviour, there are techniques which can be helpful with the student's consent and a desire to change by this method. In the school, a change can be brought about simply by a change in the behaviour of the teacher towards the student. This change can be from being critical and punitive, to being positive and encouraging. Under these conditions change for the better would not be surprising. The reinforcement aspects of behaviour modification can be applied easily in a school situation since they mean no more than a maintenance of the supportive attitude to the students and providing the same rewards that are given to other students.

There are many ways of changing things for the better. It is very rare for the problem to lie solely in the student; problems are the consequence of many strands coming into conjunction of which teachers will always be a factor.

8
HELPING OTHERS (2): COLLEAGUES

● Responsibility for emotional well-being in the school ● Ways of caring ● Quality of life among staff ● Handling the politics of school life ● Collective help among teachers ● Personal help

RESPONSIBILITY FOR
EMOTIONAL WELL-BEING IN THE SCHOOL

Teachers usually like to think of schools as communities, places where there is a community of interest and where people help one another to do things. Primary schools find it easier than secondary schools to function as whole communities largely by virtue of their smaller size, but secondary schools too can have a strong sense of community because the students are mature enough to play a responsible part in promoting and supporting activities.

Teachers also like to think of schools as caring places and would probably be offended and upset if it were suggested that the school was uncaring. But caring is an active matter; it does not just happen because we would like it to. Schools have to develop structures that ensure that caring takes place in the ways that meet the various needs. In school terminology this is done most commonly by means of the pastoral system but it invariably relates to the students and not to the teachers. Teachers are generally considered not to require pastoral care even though teacher-need and pupil-need cannot be separated.

In many ways the head is the key figure in any system of caring for staff in the same way as teachers are the key figures in caring for students. It could be argued that a good management model for the school is for the head to feel pastorally responsible for his or her colleagues while delegating to them responsibility for the students. At any rate, if heads do not accept responsibility for the care of their colleagues (teaching and non-teaching, of course) there is a large gap in the management system that has to be filled somehow. Indeed, the best way of thinking about management structures is to see them as linking levels of an organization rather than as a single longitudinal dimension of power.

> The quality of relationships between teachers and students will in a large measure depend on the quality of relationships between head and teachers. If the head holds colleagues in low esteem they will be much less motivated to relate well to the students.

The caring process

Caring is not an inevitable consequence of administrative structures but takes place at the affective level of an organization. However well everyone works at the tasks of the school, as they are expressed in material terms, if the collective spirit is missing, the tasks will contribute little to the quality of feelings of those involved. That is not to say tasks are unimportant − nothing can be achieved without them − but the most efficient way of completing tasks is in the right emotional context and frame of mind; this is normally what we call the *process* when talking about organizational behaviour.

Since the process provides the context in which a task is performed, attention to the process is a precondition to successful performance and completion of a task. Many schools are more concerned with the tasks themselves than the feelings of the people performing them with the consequence that when difficulties arise they cannot be solved easily because emotional blockages have developed.

One of the casualties of many attempts to be efficient is the emotional well-being of members. Schools need to spend a great deal of time creating the emotional conditions in which the tasks of the school can be done effectively; perhaps this is the difference between efficiency and effectiveness.

Suspension of criticism

Many schools take for granted the relationships among teachers, assuming that they are good and if not that there is little that can be done about them. The primary condition for being able to be helpful is that the helpers should be able to accept the legitimacy of the problem presented to them. Some heads defend themselves against problems by simply closing their minds to the possibility of their existence. With such an attitude the problems do not go away, they simply go underground and get worse.

Trained counsellors and others in the helping professions accept a problem from a client without moral judgement but teachers often find it difficult to suspend moral judgement because they believe that one of the functions of the school is to uphold conventional moral standards. This is one reason trained school counsellors sometimes have problems because they are perceived to be condoning immoral or illegal behaviour and getting away with it. They are sometimes considered to be subversive of what the school stands for and some heads have abandoned official counselling as a consequence.

It is perhaps the question of being judgemental that is at the heart of the difficulties for many heads and teachers when faced with behaviour of which they disapprove. The climate of many schools is often one of essential disapproval. A teacher is more likely to say, 'Jason, your tie is undone; put it straight,' than 'Jason, you're looking very smart today; your tie like that makes you look very summery.' Many schools are obsessed with finding fault with student dress but take few pains to help students to a positive self-image in the way they dress.

> It is a good personal tactic to try to say something good about a person when starting a conversation; always look for something to praise and avoid following it with criticism.

Few of us would refuse help if we were asked but it is often difficult to offer it unasked. If you are used to offering help it is easier than if you are unpractised. So it is useful to remind ourselves of the need to be positively helpful in as many ways as we can. Offering help in practical matters is always easier than it is with emotional problems.

Some people find offering help so painful that they actively avoid it – so compounding their difficulty. They bury their head in a newspaper or find something urgent to do when there seems likely to be an emotional demand made of them. Some people are so eager to help they become a menace and force people into problems they do not have. There can be a lot of unobtrusive helping that goes unnoticed and meets real need.

> One should never be too proud to ask for help and never so diffident as to refuse it.

Teachers who are caring of students will almost certainly be caring of their colleagues. Notice who opens doors for whom in the school; it tells you a lot about people.

Helping people to share

If you find the climate of your school is uncaring, one way of helping to change it is to start asking for help, not by being very demanding — and certainly not by fabricating needs — but in areas where you believe others can be drawn out. Questions about cars or gardening, home-decorating and holiday routes will draw advice from most people. It is a way of rehearsing them in being helpful. Another way is to take extra care of the places you use — bring in plants for your classroom and the staff room. Put up pictures here and there; arrange a display in the entrance hall. Heads and those with a room for their own use can make use of furnishings (an easy chair, a coffee table) and provide a drink as ways of helping people to feel at ease and ready to open up in conversation. The creation of an atmosphere of friendliness and informality is an encouragement that allows people to be more responsive and will make it easier for them to talk if they wish. If you know a colleague has something on their mind the way can be prepared by a little opening up of yourself on the same or a related issue.

> Make time, and make it clear that time is available, if there is some listening to do.

WAYS OF CARING

Time and the causes of fatigue

Perhaps the most difficult aspect of the life of any school is the sense of rush and haste. Having enough time seems a rare occurrence in most schools except towards the end of the summer term. It seems as if teachers are afraid of loose time and must fill every moment with tasks to be done. Idleness is apparently a great sin; certainly it is a great obsession. Why are teachers so afraid of time? Why do they so easily talk of time being wasted? Students are rushed from classroom to classroom; bells ring and everything stops for several minutes before another set of jobs is started. Perhaps teachers are so afraid of time just because they never finish anything; and because they never finish anything they increase their fear of wasting time. It is by no means clear how time can be wasted since no one posseses it; after all time passes whether we think about it or not. Teachers worry about lateness though being late does not seem to do anyone much harm except on the rarest of occasions.

Teachers are not themselves especially good at planning and the structure of most school timetables uses time very inefficiently and in-effectively since the allocation of time is largely irrelevant to what is done with it. When it comes to their own work, teachers seem always to be short of time to prepare, to think, to plan and to look into the future. A lot of time is spent in 'urgent' and 'pressing' tasks but very little on coming to grips with the significance of time in the organization of the school. Teachers also have so much to do that it is no wonder there is such a high level of fatigue at the end of the week and the end of the term.

Many teachers complain that it takes several days to unwind at the end of term which seems to suggest they are overdoing it during the term. One reason for this might be that secondary schools are preoccupied with co-ordinating and regulating in some detail the behaviour of a lot of people at the same time. In a secondary school once a bell rings as many as two thousand students might begin to move around. It is quite remark-able how secondary schools manage to cope with the movements of so many people. There are not many organizations other than railway stations and exhibitions that try to control so many people in so detailed a way. In normal circumstances such movement and control are rare and it is more than likely that both the movement and the reasons for it are a cause of stress, though in different ways, to a great many people. It may also be a great reliever of stress to many people who welcome the chance to change from an uncomfortable situation to another more congenial one.

If schools would cut down the organized activity there would be more opportunity for the creation of personal space and more opportunity for people to listen to one another. Excessive movement is a form of neurotic behaviour in the same way as excessive inactivity may be the consequence of an emotional state.

Schools that use block timetabling have found a way of creating more time and more opportunity for listening. Longer blocks of time take away some of the frenzy from lessons.

Where schools adopt modular courses, however, they may lose out on the potential for leisure by packing more content into more limited time spaces.

Timing of help

One of the difficulties of helping is finding the appropriate moment to intervene. Sometimes it is impossible to find the right moment and an offer of help is rejected that would have been accepted at a more opportune time. Help is best offered by simply being around when it is needed; it is not always necessary to open up the subject, merely being ready to listen is enough. The best advice about giving advice is never to give it unasked. Sometimes a little gentle exploring of possibilities is helpful and some people, if we know them well, respond better to a little coaxing; but caution cannot be overdone with strangers. Broadly speaking, if matters go undealt with they will get worse.

Many problems are worse only in so far as they seem worse the longer they are left unexplored. But with serious matters delay can be disastrous and dealing with it will be more complicated. The secret lies in being able to discriminate between the serious and ordinary. It is true that some problems will go away of their own accord and it is important not to create them where they did not exist. On the whole it is better to try to help than to let things go; if we are rebuffed it is no great hardship.

It is not only the timing but the manner of an intervention that is important. Giving yourself time to deal with the concern is part of the manner, the process; sense of timing is a function of our personal life style. We should avoid trying to help someone with a problem that is similar to one we have ourselves and which is unresolved for us. Counselling is not a way of solving your own problems through others, though that is what many people try to do. On the other hand experience of the problem area can be useful.

For example, it is easier to say the right thing in a case of bereavement if you have known a similar bereavement yourself. Self-help groups are effective because they are organized around the victims (e.g. of rape) or sufferers (e.g. drug-takers) helping one another. On the whole, the more detached the counsellor is from the problem the better. Empathy is a product of our previous experience just as much as our current experience and is probably more important than sympathy, which suggests a concurrently similar experience. By being emotionally detached from the colleague whom we are counselling we do not confuse our own feelings and theirs. If we find ourselves being drawn into the problem we have to seek additional assistance.

Intervention and confrontation

There are issues, however, in all schools where we are part of the problem and are yet unaware of it. This will be true for heads so far as many school problems are concerned. The more there are who are responsible to us, the more potentially involved we will be with organizational problems.

One of the great illusions of administrators and many managers who see themselves as good administrators is that management separates the manager from the problems of the organization. If this were so there would be little point in managing anyway, but the argument seems to be that once a good system is set up it is the fault of others if it does not work. The reason for this view is that such managers need power but use their power to distance themselves from those over whom they are in charge. The reality is that no managers can increase their distance from their colleagues by increasing their power over them; only by decreasing their power can they give them the freedom to be responsible for themselves.

Sometimes it is necessary for a head to face a colleague over some action of which he or she disapproves; in such circumstances it is difficult to be totally objective, especially about where we are ourselves in the matter. It helps if we can be accepting of what is said to us about ourselves and to explore why others feel about us as they do without trying to be defensive. When we get uptight about criticism of ourselves we are in a state of stress. We all need training to be able to face up to other people effectively and the higher up in an organization our position is the more important it is.

If we have to confront a colleague we should confront on neutral territory or on our colleague's (adversary's?) ground. Heads can easily forget how forbidding their study can be for some teachers. We need to make sure that there is ample time for a full discussion. Too often heads choose an opportunity for a difficult discussion when there is just not time for a full exploration. We should remember that we never know enough of a story beforehand to be able to make a judgement. Even if the issue seems clear to us it may not be so to our colleague. We are all of us prone to have closed minds, the more so when we are on weak grounds.

QUALITY OF LIFE AMONG STAFF

Social life of the staff room

As well as the formal help discussed so far there is a great deal of informal help and caring that is possible. We mentioned earlier the improvement of the environment with flowers, etc. but there is also the generation of activities which are themselves supportive and may be instituted simply for that reason. Inviting friends and colleagues to dinner or for drinks is one way but it can also be done at school to mark special occasions.

The general social life of the staff room is important not only because it leads to the prevention of problems but because it provides informal occasions for their resolution. Because of the lack of contact between teachers when they are in the classroom, an active social life for staff is essential to the good running of the school. Eating and drinking together are important symbols of community and help to build the community spirit.

While social demands may become excessive for some people there is a minimum that each organization requires. Indeed, the quality of social activity is a measure of the morale of the school. There should be a minimum of two social events each term – at the beginning and at the end. They should preferably be more than a perfunctory glass of sherry in the staff room, though that is better than nothing. A similar pattern should characterize the organization of each department or section. In many schools the organization of staff social events is left to the staff but it is too important to leave it to chance and it should be seen as an integral part of management though the head may do little more than act as an active facilitator; this is the easiest form of delegation.

Many schools have staff rooms that are deplorable in their untidiness, though many primary schools do not even have a separate staff room. It may be that school staff rooms are an indication of the quality of self-regard the staff have for themselves, but it is equally likely that it is a reflection of the regard they feel the local authority has for them. Teachers do not have enough personal space for belongings and the rest room usually doubles as a work room and passenger lounge. Certainly staff accommodation in most schools leaves very much to be desired and it should be of major concern to the head to see that provision is adequate.

Some heads deny responsibility by saying that the staff room belongs to the staff and that they therefore keep out unless invited in. This says something sad about the relationship of heads to their colleagues and deserves fuller examination in the school.

Teachers do seem to produce a lot of clutter and to encourage one another to do so. They are exceedingly tolerant of one another's clutter, too, perhaps because they are protecting themselves for the (frequent) times when they have piles of materials and nowhere to put them. Some people are only happy in clutter; unfortunately clutter soon becomes filth.

There seem to be five activities that should be separately provided for but which have become confused in most schools. They are: eating and drinking; relaxing and conversing; marking and preparation; meeting for business purposes; and private space for confidential matters, interviewing visitors, etc. Schools need to give consideration to the quality of space available to both staff and students, for students are always worse off than teachers in this regard.

Too many schools have a general appearance of neglect and it cannot all be due to inadequate local authority funding. People tend to accept the physical conditions of the work place without doing much about it except for minor embellishments and pasting up pictures of one sort or another. Significantly, physical conditions improve as you move up the hierarchy and the mere fact of such distinctions indicates the managerial philosophy of the school. A good starting place of discovering the truth about a school is the state of the lavatory and washing facilities.

Organizational depression

A consequence of the hurried pace of life of schools is a dulling of awareness not only of physical conditions but of social relationships. Among the classic symptoms of depression are carelessness in dress, a dulled sensitivity to oneself and to others, and a general lack of environmental awareness. These are characteristics of many schools; schools can be depressing places because the teachers are themselves depressed. School depression is endemic in many forms. Depressed individuals curtail their relationships with other people and sometimes become aggressive in interpersonal relationships. It may become diffused into a general anomie, alienation or aggressiveness. The causes are many and include teacher frustration, perceived lack of resources, incompetence in teaching, unrealistic expectations, emotional sickness (especially of the head), lack of a sense of achievement.

One of the pervasive causes of depression arises from the very vagueness of purposes or objectives of schools. Unlike any other kind of organization public or private (except perhaps churches) schools cannot have clear purposes or objectives but must serve at a remove the various unclear expectations of everyone they relate to. Schools are inevitably social conveniences and have to serve too many masters. A consequence of this is that they are tempted to claim too much for themselves.

We would have to live in a remarkably unified society for the schools to be able to fulfil all the requirements of parents in a multicultural society; for the United Kingdom was multicultural even before ethnic minorities were considered important. One reason the old-fashioned grammar school appeared to be successful (though opinions about this vary) was that it attempted so little and could (appear to) achieve it.

> Given that everyone has their own idea of what the school should do, little wonder no one can ever manage to do it. It is no surprise teachers often have such low morale when they have so many masters to please.

Additionally, there is the problem of the discrepancy between what the individual teacher wants for the school and what the school organization is designed to achieve. Most secondary schools are still organized basically for public examinations yet many teachers will claim that personal development and the acquisiton of life and work skills is more important. They will even go so far as to say examinations are unimportant so long as students learn how to cope with getting or not getting a job and relating to other people in society. The discrepancy is further compounded because most teachers will 'do their own thing' in the classroom whatever the requirements of the school organization – the traditional freedom of the teacher in the classroom.

There can be little doubt that teachers find themselves in a maelstrom of uncertainty in which the qualities least valued are their personal ones for even in the proverbial qualifications-orientated system it is the teacher who is seen as the failure in the end not the pupils. Because teachers find themselves working in a system that cannot provide for them in the way their emotional and intellectual needs require, there can be little wonder that stress is a continuing problem.

HANDLING THE POLITICS OF SCHOOL LIFE

Because teachers are operationally unsophisticated about organizational politics, they usually fail to recognize political situations in school and, when they do, they do not have the skills for dealing with them. Teacher unions, for example, have until quite recently played little part in the politics of the school but choose to function at a different level. Union membership is not based on organizational divisions but on ideological grounds and preferred modes of confrontation. There are no mechanisms in (most?) schools for dealing with issues of internal power/politics; indeed it is assumed that teachers and management have an identity of interest which they probably do not have. Staff meetings are conducted on the basis of there not being any significant conflict of interests and if they do exist then they ought not to. The effect of this is that schools never tackle issues of conflict — presumably because the great unfaceable is that students might have organizational rights too. By and large the head is final arbiter and other teachers have at best advisory rights.

The key to understanding the management reality of any school is to look at how the heads of department view themselves managerially; most of them do not see themselves as managers and they are not treated as such. In recent years more heads have come to treat heads of department as middle managers but most of them find the confusion between being a manager and being a teacher too confusing, which is hardly surprising since many heads also find it impossible. Of course, school departments are quite small by some standards but in the further education sector, heads of department have always been thought of as managers and in industry supervisors may be in charge of fewer people than even a medium-sized school department. At any rate, uncertainty over the nature of the 'real' job is a cause of stress.

Given that schools are confused about what they are supposed to be doing and that the problem is unsolvable in the present political climate, the only solution open to individuals is to determine for themselves what they want to do and to go about doing it. This sounds remarkably like being responsible for oneself and it is the one sure way to avoid stress, at least in its extreme forms. Teachers who are forever looking over their shoulder for someone else's appraisal of them are asking for trouble. Understanding organizations better will help.

COLLECTIVE HELP AMONG TEACHERS

Different modes for different people

For close friends who are colleagues the ways that we can help may be very different from the ways that we can help another member of staff with whom we have little contact. As we elaborate earlier, three different levels of coping are possible: organizational, interpersonal and personal. We can help colleagues on all three levels. The notion of the timing of different sorts of coping is relevant here and links to different types of stress.

The diagram shows stress analysed along two dimensions of intensity and changeability. Some stresses are difficult, though not impossible, to change, for example those that may arise from timetabling arrangements.

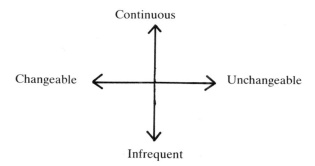

Some stress, although minor, may be continuous and wear away the teacher like water dripping onto rock, while others might have a shock effect due to the lack of warning and suddenness. Some forms of coping may be preventive ensuring that the event does not happen or that its effects may be minimized. For example, if a school were due to close, certain procedures and consultations would ensure that most teachers felt a minimum of stress from the exercise. In fact, we know these situations are not managed well and high stress levels often result.

Clearly many situations that are likely to cause stress in teachers could be prevented from happening by changes being made before the event. Some of these changes could be simple and straightforward but all too often inertia or, worse, complacency dictates the continuation of established rituals and routines. If situations can be avoided some forethought would enable negative consequences to be predicted which would in turn enable positive ways of avoiding the negative consequences to be sorted out. Problems usually occur because the situation is seen as inevitable but even with considerable disasters good management will help to avoid additional problems of stress.

Group support

At the interpersonal level, group support is the main way of supporting colleagues. There are two major ways of coping better; one is to reduce the sources of stress and the other is to increase sources of help, including personal resources. It is usually desirable to do both and maximize the effects. This implies a good knowledge of the situation. Groups can be a very valuable way of enabling people to seek help and support particularly if they meet regularly and include caring in their agenda. This may easily revolve around an informal social gathering. An example of this is a group who meet on Monday lunch times and take it in turns to provide a snack lunch. It enables each member to contribute to the food, but infrequently, and provides a relaxed atmosphere within which to share problems and look for group support.

Groups and quality circles

Another form of group support is *quality circles*, a form of problem-solving group used in industry. The range of group functions can be considerable including tackling problems that are related to teaching in a particular subject area to the development of specialist skills with group support. Quality circles are used to monitor the quality of work of an industrial work group and to harness the skills and insights of the workers themselves in solving practical problems they face in their daily work. They make recommendations to management which management take on board and do something about. They have been used in some large schools in an adapted form. The important factor in their success is that all members have equal status. They may undertake a series of investigations to find solutions to their problems and their brief is entirely pragmatic.

Such activities have profound implications for the management of stress in the groups and the ways individuals cope. A teacher in such a group may initially lack confidence, by working closely together with colleagues confidence will be gained. Such groups may also take on the role of counselling individuals about their job performance. One factor about groups is that they are always different even if they are dynamically basically the same. They change to meet the needs of members rather than moving towards being some ideal type.

Many informal groups exist in schools, sometimes based upon friendship patterns or on shared interests. The importance of these groups is that they provide an emotional support which can be drawn on in times of trouble. The pity is there is so little time available in the normal day for them to function. Within them colleagues can relax and feel easy with themselves. They tend to be places of good humour and high spirits.

> Humour is a good morale booster for it is often directed against a common enemy. Humour is at its healthiest when it is directed at the humourist's own group and the joker personally.

PERSONAL HELP

Any means of supporting a colleague is helpful so long as it is perceived as such. Sometimes we try too hard to help or we help in too fussy a way. Sometimes we offer help when it is unwelcome but nevertheless it is better to try than not to try. Crisis occurs when stress is unresolved. We may be unable to concentrate on our work, become solitary or insensitive, unable to interact positively with our colleagues except when sharing our problems. In such circumstances we may become suggestible to other's influence.

> People are particularly vulnerable to suggestion when in a low emotional state. Be careful what you suggest to them about their condition.

Collusion as support

Moral support is the kind that provides confirmation that our actions are reasonable and acceptable to our peers. A teacher may receive strong moral support from colleagues for vigorously upbraiding a pupil for a minor misdemeanour even though the parents make a justifiable formal complaint. Usually extenuating circumstances are pleaded and accepted as sufficient by colleagues even though there may be doubts as to the correctness of the teacher's actions. Teachers tend to support one another even when in the wrong in order to reinforce the solidarity of the profession. A typical example is the way teachers collude in support of a colleague against students, however unreasonably they may have behaved.

Another form of affirmation which is an important aspect of moral support is the recognition that problems exist and that some are serious; in other words, the teacher is right to be concerned and to seek help.

Teachers are often very hesitant to voice their fears and anxieties in school and may struggle with very difficult situations before making tentative moves to make it public. The problem should not arise in a truly caring community because members would feel free to share anxieties at an early stage. In ordinary school circumstances, teachers feel a sense of shame or even guilt at exposing their difficulties and will need all the help they can get to overcome it.

Feedback can be a mixed blessing to the teacher. Positive feedback is rarely given and negative feedback increases anxiety and stress in such a way it may make it more difficult for the stressed individual to change. One way of enhancing our social environment is by being very pleasant and saying nice things about one another. Giving praise is not part of the norms of most schools so a special effort must be made. For example, after a difficult lesson a teacher could be given positive feedback about how well they managed and pointing up the good things that happened.

Another way of helping teachers to cope better is by questioning and challenge. This happens more than may be realized but is not at all systematic. A teacher may express feelings of being fed up but when colleagues question these feelings they find there is another emotion, such as having to face an unruly class or difficulty in teaching to a certain level. Asking a question or issuing a challenge enables speakers to evaluate what they have said. Sometimes people feel pinned down or trapped by being questioned because it feels like being interrogated. This will occur when the questioner forgets the purpose of the questioning which is to assist insight.

The second major purpose of questioning is to enable you to consider aspects of the case which may have eluded you, to place the situation in a different perspective. For example, you may be upset by an incident but on consideration you see it to be quite normal and almost routine. The questioner can point out the means of help available so that you can make your own evaluation. Teachers are likely to find this sort of questioning difficult because they tend to use questions for different purposes − to check learning, for example − and they may ask questions only to receive direct answers rather than enlightenment.

The values of humour

We have mentioned humour briefly as a means of coping with anxiety. When a situation is very threatening, 'black humour' is often employed. Teachers laugh at pupils and they laugh at politicians and the local authority; they make jokes because they cannot reach their target and laughter assuages the hurt. Students make jokes, too, about their difficulties and about their teachers on whom they cannot revenge themselves. Parents, educational psychologists, visiting professionals such as college lecturers all become the butt of jokes. Teachers also laugh about themselves.

All such laughter is healthy if it helps the humourists to cope better but unhealthy if it leads to greater obsessiveness. If we cannot laugh at ourselves we are in a parlous state because we will become pompous and irrational. Above all humour is infectious and makes others take themselves less seriously. There is nothing like laughter for relieving tension. Once we see the funny side of a problem it becomes manageable and we see it in a softer, less-threatening light.

If you are a sympathetic but jokey person you may well be sought out as pleasant and supportive company. Often we are far too serious when trying to help our colleagues with problems and sometimes we make the problems much worse by taking them too seriously. Not every problem turns out to be serious even if it is potentially so. Helping others to keep a sense of proportion requires us to keep a sense of proportion ourselves. If we are too serious we misjudge the level on which matters can be put right.

9
CAREERS AND AMBITION

● Developing a sense of professional identity ● Personal style as a teacher ● Personality and job performance ● Self-appraisal ● Ambition and the prospect of promotion ● Re-evaluating expectations ● Coping with unhappiness in teaching ● Family, home and friendships

DEVELOPING A SENSE
OF PROFESSIONAL IDENTITY

There must be a whole lot of reasons why people take up teaching and they are probably not very different from the reasons people take up any job. Teaching has generally been thought of as the sort of job one takes for life, a profession. Once a teacher starts on a teaching career the way ahead is gently marked out. For men it offers a secure (at least until recently) and socially useful job with some social status particularly if he achieves a headship. For women it offers much the same prospects but with the advantage for married women of being the sort of job one could go back to. In the 1960s hosts of women were recruited into the profession largely on the basis of its convenience for married women.

The commonest rewards have always been held to be the long holidays which compensate for low pay, and the short hours — although of late it has become customary to deny this in public. People take up teaching because they see it as a rewarding job in the personal sense and because it seems to suit their lifestyle. The trouble is that teachers are becoming more and more disillusioned with their job. There are many examples of breakdown or burnout and a significant number take premature early retirement or simply, if they are under 50, leave for another job (usually to run a small business or sell insurance).

Teachers talk a good deal about their 'profession' and there is little doubt that most teachers see their occupation as 'more than just a job'. Most teachers see themselves as professionals who take the performance of their job very seriously. This means that they put themselves under a great deal of pressure to behave according to certain ethical criteria, even if these criteria are not explicit.

There is among teachers a strong but undefined sense of duty though it is not entirely shared by their superiors in the administrative system. The concept of professionalism is further complicated by the difficulty of defining teaching — Is it instruction, socialization, facilitation, coaching, childminding or what? Added to this is the idea that teachers are in some way in loco parentis and the position becomes even less clear as to what are appropriate criteria for judging performance.

The salary structure to teaching with its limited scale of rewards suggests a professional orientation but the managerial aspects of the educational service indicate that the poor incentive structure does not work well. The teachers' unions themselves seem to be ambiguous about whether there ought to be a single career grade or there ought to be a more flexible and creative structure.

Teaching and parenting

It is perhaps the concepts of 'teacher' and 'parent' that create most problems in the development of professional identity for teachers. On the one hand, they see themselves as holding the children in trust for their parents and as such being responsible for upholding the values of the home. On the other hand, they believe that the job of the teacher is to enrich the lives of their students and help them to move beyond the limitations of their upbringing. Most teachers would consider that education is a broadening experience without wondering too much whether this causes conflict between what parents would wish and what teachers believe important for the child.

Teachers who look to their role as an extension of parenting may find themselves more stressed than those who see themselves as instructors but they may also find themselves more satisfied. Parenting

> attitudes on the part of the teacher are not wrong but are more
> likely to bring teachers into conflict with parents because they
> become rivals.

Adopting a parenting role means that teachers take on more responsibilities than they can cope with. This is particularly true in special
education where teaching tasks can overlap considerably with parents'
tasks. Whatever job anyone has it is necessary to distinguish personal
involvement and personal identification. In the one situation there is
sufficient psychological distancing to hold the job at bay; but in the
second there is danger of so identifying with the job that it becomes an
extension of one's personal life. In organizational terms the first will
cause less stress than the second.

PERSONAL STYLE AS A TEACHER

However well the tasks of a job may be defined, the way in which they
are performed is a matter of personal choice. In practice all jobs have
some negotiable areas as to how they are done, even if what is done is
fairly inflexible. Generally we choose a job because of what is required to
be done rather than how, but having once started work it soon becomes
clear that there are many 'hows' and the choice is exceedingly personal. If
we do not like how we are to do a job we try to change it to where the
manner of performing it is acceptable.

Perhaps strangely we may put ourselves under less stress in the job we
do not like than in the one we do like. For if we do not like a job we will
probably take it less seriously and put less effort into it. Quite often
teachers are not aware just how strong is the encouragement to conform
to certain ways of doing things in school. Only when they change schools
do they realize that their previous job was burdensome.

On the whole, however, the generally expressed view is that teaching is
one of those (few?) jobs where there is a lot of choice as to not only how
you do it but what you do. The proverbial idea is of teachers as rulers of
their own kingdom of the classroom. Presumably this is one of the
attractions of teaching as a profession.

To exercise choice one must be informed about the matters among
which one is choosing and in teaching this is less clear than ever it was. It
used to be that choice of teaching style was simply a matter of self-
expression or a straightforward alternative mode like direct method for
teaching modern languages as against a textbook approach. But nowadays

there are so many fundamentally different modes of teaching that an established teacher must be bewildered for so many experts come into the school from outside or from other sectors. The current developments in TVEI (Technical and Vocational Education Initiative) and MSC courses are enough to disturb the complacency of secondary-school teachers but do not help them to solve the problems of school organization and examinations – all the more difficult with a single school-leaving examination, GCSE.

If teachers once upon a time felt that they would be left alone in the classroom to do more or less what they liked, this is no longer the case. The threat of teacher appraisal will never go away. The demand to change is very exacting because it requires whole new views of the nature of classroom activity let alone the concept of education. The common response to all this is often emotional withdrawal in one way or another.

Even freedom within your own classroom is not so free of stress as is sometimes thought. Any enthusiastic or even moderately responsible teacher will want to exploit the opportunities of the classroom and that means you will do more and more over and above the bare necessities. Gradually the demands build up, accumulating from year to year until teachers finds themselves under constraint to do things because they were done the year previously and with success.

Historically, teachers have taken on all sorts of jobs as natural extensions of classroom activity which have now become unbearably burdensome and material for political bargaining – supervision of school meals, parents' evenings, out-of-school activities, training courses are now all to be excluded from normal working.

Probably teachers have always tried to do more for the students than was strictly necessary though there is no means of knowing what that *necessary* is. Indeed, it may be that those activities not part of the standard curriculum are the most helpful. At any rate, no doubt the reason teachers have traditionally done so much for students out of school is that they found these activities quite as rewarding as – and probably more so – formal classroom activity.

Problems of choice

The problem appears to have two major causes. One is that schools do not have clear and simple organizational objectives or purposes and the other is that teachers often do not know what they want to do themselves. Schools are locations of generalized collective activity (education) rather than specific technical and mechanical processes even when basic skills are being taught. Once the very general purposes of education have been expressed (and this will always be some sort of compromise and aggregation) there are great problems in reducing them to simple operational objectives applicable to each student; even the teaching of reading, writing and computation are virtually open-ended. When such ideas as moral judgement, aesthetic experience and spiritual awareness are added, the difficulties for evaluation and assessment are insuperable.

It is proper that schools should not have simple organizational objectives because this would make it even more difficult to accommodate individual student needs. Without customers in the commercial sense schools cannot have objectives other than of a pragmatic kind.

For teachers who are under stress, the existence of very clear objectives and purposes may not be helpful because it would increase the sense of obligation to do what is impossible.

There is a degree of difference between individuals choosing rational objectives for themselves and having to abide by objectives chosen with some ambiguity by others and declared to be valid for the whole organization.

PERSONALITY AND JOB PERFORMANCE

Personality and growth

There are two basic factors that may determine our response to a job. One is our personality and the other is the expectations we have of the job. The two are linked; in career terms we choose a job because we believe it will suit our personality. Personality is a difficult concept (especially for psychologists). Broadly speaking it is a description of the kind of person we are as other people experience it but it is also the idea we have of ourself, our self-concept as we have termed it in this book.

It is unlikely that our personality changes much but it undoubtedly develops as the years go by and we are influenced by the experience of life that we have. On the whole it tends to be consistent in that our friends easily recognize our behaviour to be characteristic of us. Our self-concept changes as we come to understand our basic self more clearly which we can do only through reflection. Levels of reflection, however, vary from person to person and from time to time. We hope that as we mature reflection becomes a more controlled process in that we are able to look carefully at ourselves with increased 'objectivity'.

On the whole we need assistance in this process of self-reflection particularly if we think badly about ourselves because then we tend to see bad things rather than good things. It is essential for us to have a positive self-concept if we are to deal with problems in life and this means that we should be realistic but optimistic about ourselves. Fortunately human beings have a great capacity for self-learning and good learning invariably leads to an improved self-concept.

It is useful for us to make a distinction between what we believe we would like out of life and the circumstances that give us pleasure and satisfaction. Often we look continually into the future in the expectation that someday everything we want will be available. When we are young we tend to look forward eagerly and sometimes unrealistically. As we get older we begin to look nearer at hand and to take enjoyment out of what is nearer to us, the daily life around us. When we are very old, we look to the past but can only do so without regret if we are still capable of enjoying the present.

Of course, the important time is always the present for that is the product of the past and the creator of the future. We need to hold in balance reasonable expectation about the future with a realistic appreciation of the present if we are to ensure that the 'future present' is right for us. There is a skilful juggling with our aspirations in terms of where we are now and where we would like to be at some time in the future. One way of doing this is to keep a monitoring watch on our career through the achievements that have current substance for us.

Whatever evaluation we make of our career, we cannot afford to regret the past or discount its importance. Few of us find ourselves at 45 feeling that we have achieved what we aspired to at 21, but we are probably all the better for that because it is likely to mean that we made a lot of good decisions at various decision points in our life; that is, decisions that were a product of our realistic self-awareness in terms of the risks we were able to take. We often look back and say 'I ought to have done so-and-so', but the fact that we did not may mean we were realistic about ourselves rather than we misjudged the situation.

On the whole teachers enjoy being with their students and feel an obligation to them which often has to take precedence over their own wishes. For instance, teachers can change their jobs only at certain times in the year but even so one time is best when the students are on a year-long course. Sometimes teachers feel themselves committed to a class of students for a two-year period or more. This all makes it difficult for teachers to plan their own future just as they would wish it and to take advantage of opportunities as they occur.

SELF-APPRAISAL

It is important for everyone in a career that involves working with people at a close emotional level — which teaching does — to take time out from time to time for self-evaluation. All work with people is stressful at some time or another because it is so easy to lose your sense of identity in constantly meeting other people's demands. A period of guided intro-spection is essential and by preference it should have an institutional element in it. By this we mean there should be someone within each school with whom you can talk about your job and appraise your feelings about it. This may or may not be as part of a formal appraisal though this would be good for everyone provided relationships among staff are sup-portive enough — democratic leadership might be of this kind. If self-appraisal can be related to membership of the school and be conducted in a supportive and creative way, it can relieve a good many of the appre-hensions that cause people to be stressed.

It should also be possible to talk informally with trusted colleagues about personal matters related to school and career. It is absolutely important for teachers to be able to find emotional support in the school in the same way that social workers and others receive support through supervision. You cannot support other people in their needs without emotional support for yourself. Teachers feel it is a sign of weakness that they should need help with any aspect of their job and many heads would not know how to give it if it were recognized. So some attention needs to be given in most schools for both formal and informal counselling about job performance and career orientation.

AMBITION AND THE PROSPECT OF PROMOTION

Ambition and striving

Teachers are often too proud to ask for help, perceiving it as an indict-ment of their own adequacy whereas in fact being able to recognize a personal need is a mature response. As we grow older and maturer we should become increasingly realistic about ourselves; we should know more clearly what works for us and what doesn't. Understanding where our satisfactions lie is one of the processes of emotional maturity. Being able to discard areas of activity where we do not receive satisfaction is also an aspect of maturity.

Contemplating promotion

One reason why many teachers want to be heads or advisers or college lecturers is that they realize that teaching young students no longer gives the satisfactions they need and so they want to press on to something different. However, there is always a difficulty when we change our job or place of work; we do not realize until we do so what were the advantages of the job until we have left it. We may have taken for granted the nearness to school that we once had until we are faced with a one-hour journey for the new post. We forget that houses in the north are cheaper than in the south until we have to sell and buy. We overlook the importance of a country school in the attitudes of the students and only realize how difficult teenagers can be when we take a promotion into a downtown school. We all make 'mistakes' of this kind and the effect can be exceedingly stressful because they are difficult to undo.

We also compound the discontent by believing that it is not acceptable to make mistakes and have regrets. Yet the best ways of coping require us to admit what is emotionally true for us and to build a coping response from there. If the move to a city school really is making us unhappy even after all the rational considerations have been thoroughly rehearsed, then we must respond to the fundamental need to be in a comfortable environment however professionally undignified we may think it is.

The likelihood is that having made a choice in our own genuine interest others around us will admire us for our self-confidence. None of us can ensure that our head always rules our heart but we can behave rationally when we really do understand our emotions.

The problem with ambition is that it has no tangibility. Whatever it is, it is an emotional state around something that we do with regard to the future. Though we can say we have at last fulfilled an ambition, we can only say so after the event, we cannot know that we will be able to say it however precisely defined our ambition may be. There is no guarantee that when we have become the head teacher, which we believe was the object of our ambition, we will be happy in the position that we actually fill. Yet without ambition of some sort we should stagnate and there would be nothing to look forward to, which for many people is one of the things that keeps them motivated.

> We should be less concerned with specific circumstances in looking towards the future and more concerned with states of mind that we find congenial.

It is unlikely that being stressed is the consequence simply of frustrated ambition, though this is not to say frustrated ambition may not be stressful – bearing in mind the lack of specificity in ambition. On the whole, people who are very ambitious are usually purposeful and fairly clear about what they want to do and how they will achieve it. Some others who mention ambition do nothing to achieve it and either lack confidence in themselves or really do not have ambition but wishful thinking.

Being successful in terms of ambition is neither stressful nor relieving of stress; successful people may be under stress as much as unsuccessful people because discontent is a state of mind not a circumstance. Being stressed is a consequence of a perception rather than a 'reality'; unsuccessful people are so because they think themselves to be unsuccessful.

We have said this frequently but it needs to be stated again in the context of ambition and career development because many teachers seem to look to a change of school to further their career and this always involves a higher degree of uncertainty in making career choices than in many other jobs where one stays with only one or two employers throughout a whole working life.

> It may be that teachers who change jobs change one set of stress-inducing circumstances for another and what they have failed to do is learn how to cope with stress in the first place. Once you develop successful coping strategies they are transferable whereas the nature of jobs may not change from place to place.

Assessment of personal satisfactions

The importance of personal appraisal is in looking carefully at what is creative and fulfilling in your life and in looking for opportunities to develop and enrich what is already there rather than looking for something completely different. In fact the road to the completely different is usually through what you already know well. The technique is to look carefully at the satisfactions currently in your life and to find ways of building on them. Alongside this is to look at areas of dissatisfaction to see if they indicate an area to be developed.

We can adopt the same process with regard to our teaching by examining what elements give us satisfaction and which leave us feeling discontented. Then we can turn the discontents to positive dispositions by finding congenial ways of dealing with them. The important fact is that whatever we do in the future is dependent on what we do now. We have to create the future for ourselves through what we do with and in our present.

RE-EVALUATING EXPECTATIONS

Dangers of teaching as compensation

Wherever our future lies, our paid employment is only a part of it. Teaching should not be the sole source of our satisfactions and it certainly should not provide satisfactions that more properly belong elsewhere. The school and the classroom are too limited to provide for all the needs of the mature adult. That is not to say teaching cannot not give plentiful satisfactions.

There is a danger that for some of us our job becomes a compensation for the failures in the rest of our life activities and it may even be seen as a sort of punishment for other failings of ourselves or our families. Total dedication to teaching may be an escape from other difficulties rather than a total fulfilment. Complete absorption in our job is limiting and stultifying; it reduces our experience and clouds our vision. Furthermore, we may take on the immaturity of the students and express them more largely and more grotesquely in our behaviour. To prepare for the future (and live in the present) that is truly ours, we need to be no slave to any institution or any body of people.

Undoubtedly some − perhaps many − teachers go out of their way to help children who are in need of special help; there has been a steady increase in the various forms of special provision over recent years. Perhaps a sense of altruism is a way of coping with difficulties for some people, but for others it may be a way of preventing a realistic appraisal of why they are in the job and what they are getting out of it. Believing you are doing something for others may be an excuse for not doing something for yourself when you ought to be.

Teachers should not feel guilty about caring for themselves and going after their own satisfactions. There is every reason to believe that when we do what is right for us it enables others to do what is right for them. We can help others best when we acknowledge our own needs; otherwise we are in danger of abusing them. We should enjoy what we teach and others are more likely to share our enjoyment. If we teach without enjoyment there can be no pleasure for our students. And so it is with those things we want to do for career's sake; so long as we know why we do them we shall harm no one.

Changing expectations

Most of us change our ideas about what we want out of life and our careers as we grow older. Sometimes the change is gradual, sometimes we are surprised with suddenness. School organization tends not to recognize that teachers' interests change but expect them to want to do the same things year after year. But teachers get bored with subjects and age groups and being in school. They need changes not always permanently but for a time. In recent years this need has come to be recognized though more out of the exigencies of falling roles than from a true realization that teachers need change. Some teachers go in for job experience or take a full-time university course; some are sent on special secondment for the local authority on some project; some manage an overseas exchange.

Rather than wait for these opportunities to come out of the blue, we should actively seek them; they are one of the best antidotes to depression available. New ones can be created if you have imagination — such as taking a year or two out to do something you have always wanted to do. In the future, there will be more turn around of teachers than ever before as teachers leave for other businesses and people from other trades and occupations take a turn at teaching. The enrichment of school life as a consequence will be therapeutic.

Those who feel they have had enough of teaching and would like to get out should not be afraid to consider doing so. There is plenty of professional counselling around that will help in the decision and the chance of leaving teaching for something else should be seen as a positive step rather than an admission of failure. There is life beyond teaching which for many people is very rewarding. Deliberately changing jobs bears no stigma but in most cases leads to unthought of contentment and challenge. If you find that the idea of leaving teaching persists and recurs, it is likely that the present discontent will only be resolved by doing so. No need for regrets.

COPING WITH UNHAPPINESS IN TEACHING

Often we feel vaguely unhappy about our job because, without having any obvious negative aspects, it just lacks positive ones. This can include a low level of demand made upon us. If this is the case, we must take greater control over our life and ensure that the necessary conditions are created both in the job itself and in related activities.

> Factors important in job satisfaction include appreciation, autonomy, comfortable environment, opportunity, good personal relationships, support, variety, complexity, significance, success, influence, and specific rewards.

However, not all of the preceding factors will apply to everyone or to any two people in the same way because we all have different concepts of happiness. There are also a number of negative factors that are generally felt to lead to dissatisfaction. They include negative consequences, demands for change, underload or overload, demands to prove ourselves, physical danger, environmental pressure, bureaucratic interference, administrative worries, guilt, emotional overextension, overdemanding deadlines, and conflicting demands from others.

Matching needs with jobs

One of the ways usually recommended for self-analysis is to consider your interests and try to match them to employment opportunities. But there are dangers in doing this since it is one thing to indulge in something for pleasure and quite another to spend your working life doing it.

> For many people pleasure is something they expect not of work but only of non-working activities.

Many people are envious of others who appear to be able to earn a good living doing something that they like, but this might well not be what actually happens. Writers, for example, rarely talk of writing as pleasurable but as hard work which makes considerable demands and can be quite uncomfortable. Professional sportsmen spend long hours in training and repetitive tasks that most people would find quite demoralizing. The process of analysis of our favourite and enjoyable activities must be realistic about both our preferences and the true nature of the jobs we examine. We can seldom do this on our own but need assistance. The two kinds available to most of us are the advice and counselling of friends and various aptitude tests available from careers guidance professionals. It is important to choose for this purpose friends who we can reasonably expect to be objective about us.

There are some concepts that we need to be clear about because they influence our choices and decisions. The first of these is character, or the kind of person we are. Some people are more temperamentally suited than others to a job even though they have similar aptitudes. For example, someone who is methodical and meticulous may make a good accountant but not a good journalist; temperament rather than skill is the critical factor. In addition, there are the particular and habitual coping strategies that we use which will vary in appropriateness from job to job.

For example, someone who copes by avoidance strategies may make a good bureaucrat because postponements will not show up so much. But coping by avoidance would be no use in a travel agency. So it may be more important to find out how you cope with stress in making job decisions than knowing what your interests are.

A second strand of personal concepts is that of skills, talents and knowledge. Quite often the skills required for a job are not the ones either advertised or looked for. At first glance we might seem to be well-qualified but on examination there are additional or even completely different other skills that are wanted.

Of course, we may not want to use all our skills in a particular job; we may want to keep them for outside work. Our skills may be classified as those with some sort of 'certification' such as examinations and tests provide or they may be skills we have gained through experience but have not been certified. Usually it is the second group that is the most valuable and for which in practice most of us are employed. In teaching, first qualifications soon become largely irrelevant yet teachers do not always take advantage of this. Quite a proportion of teachers do not teach the subject they qualified in. The importance of experience over qualifications is even greater outside the traditional professions.

Another relevant factor is the framework of your life. From time to time it is useful to make an assessment of what matters in our life and what does not. For some people, living in the country is the most important element in their life frame and they welcome the long drive to work because it puts work and home at a comfortable distance. For someone else the long drive would be the most stressful part of the day and living within walking distance of school (whether in town or country, no matter) would be the most restful circumstance. Included in this framework are such things as family configuration (where members of the family live in relation to one another), friendship patterns, hobbies and interests which are more appropriate to some areas than others, life routines in general (gardening, shopping, entertainment, travel, health needs).

FAMILY, HOME AND FRIENDSHIPS

One of the difficulties in contemplating change is that several factors will be changed too, not just the ones that are the most stressful. If families are moved there will almost certainly be complications for everyone, with someone coming out of it badly, at least for a time. Perhaps the aspect of life frame most overlooked is the relationships among the family; often they are taken for granted and their values not appreciated until too late.

Characteristics of a cohesive family

The importance of family support where the family is a cohesive unit cannot be over-emphasized. There is more time spent in shared activities in the family, and less withdrawal, avoidance of segregation of individual members. Members of the family communicate more fully and more accurately with each other and the interactions are likely to be warm with a lower rate of hostile or critical reactions. Indeed, there is generally a more favourable evaluation of members and a lower level of criticism of others. This is reflected in the perception of most family members that others in the family have a favourable view of them. Members of a cohesive family are likely to have better morale and greater optimism about the future of the family group and to show a higher level of affection.

One major benefit of being a member of a cohesive family is that you are supported without the family itself breaking down. In other words, the family is strong as a dynamic unit. But what effects will a change in employment have on the family? Will you be away from home for longer periods and more frequently? What will the financial implications be? How will holiday arrangements be affected? How will family arrangements for children and parents be changed? Will there be transport implications? (Another car needed?) The question of moving house might arise even with a fairly local change of job.

It is a good idea to look at the implications systematically and to draw up a kind of 'profit and loss' inventory as a means of giving full consideration to possible changes. The truth is that even when the job we are in is a cause of stress, the move itself to another position is a stressful experience and may be cumulative if there are other stressors in our life at the time. Yet job changes of one sort or another are characteristic of teaching and require to be viewed in the most positive and constructive ways.

Friendships

Job changes affect not only family relationships and dynamics but also friendship patterns. Generally speaking, if we move house with a new job we have to establish new friendships. Rarely do friendships endure changes that involve great distances, though for all of us some will continue in an intermittent way. The matter is made more complicated because a lot of friendship patterns are based on work even if not directly with those we work with. Often we rely on contacts at the work place to meet people we become friendly with because there is a starting point of some substance in that we do at least work in the same place and are more likely to have a commonality of interest.

A change of job can mean the loss of many social contacts which we have taken for granted but it may also mean the loss of a well-developed social support network. It is easy to forget that many people we consider our friends are in fact so just because we have working contact. They provide us with essential social and psychological support without our having to make too much effort to ask for it. And we may be providing the same kind of support to others without being too aware of that either. But when the job ends, so do these contacts unless we are able to make a special and warranted effort to maintain them. But if we do maintain them, they have a different function from previously and occur in a different context. Such earlier friendships can be very helpful in our adjustment to a new job by providing listening ears of people who know us well and understand our reactions to situations.

Another area where friendship patterns may change is in recreational activities. Hobbies and interests are often the basis for friendship development. It is important to evaluate how important our leisure interests are when deciding on a new job because not all activities can be followed in a new social situation. If we love sea fishing it might not be a very good idea to take a job in the West Midlands.

Sometimes we are not aware how important our interests and hobbies are in helping us to cope. A large garden might be a great chore but we may find that that is why we are able to relax from work; a smaller garden would leave us too much time to worry about work. Our social interests can provide us with alternative perspectives on life which help us to look at work more realistically. The quality of our lives can be heightened considerably by the exercise of skills in non-work areas and can directly influence our work performance and thus our experience of stress and coping skills.

Healthy lifestyle

Living a healthy lifestyle is a precursor to coping. Not everyone we know who leads a useful and creative life also lives a healthy life, of course. The effects of careless living always show and we need to look carefully at the bad habits — usually of neglect — we allow ourselves to fall into. One effect of job changes whether or not affected by house changes is that our routines are interrupted and we may find it difficult to recapture good habits. Whereas it was once easy to go for an evening walk to post a letter and take a circuitous route, in the new job we finish too late and want just to flop in front of the television. Or the pleasant lamp-lit streets of the town where walking to the shops was necessitated by parking difficulties is replaced by a car drive every time you want to leave the shopless country village.

It is worth taking some time to plan a healthy lifestyle when taking up a new job as well as developing the best ways of working. A new job has these two parallel but interdependent challenges. Above all, you should make time during the day for healthy pursuits — taking real lunch-time breaks and going for a walk or a swim if possible not just marking books.

In other words, personal well-being is essential to sustain any change in life circumstance. Sometimes, the felt need to another job is no more than a desire to disentangle the problems in the present one. By becoming too enmeshed in the job we have, we seek another one as the only way out. We may or may not be right to do so but our ability to cope with the one job or the other will still depend on the quality of our physical life; low morale and poor health are closely related, the one is the complement of the other.

If you have a good sense of well-being you are likely to feel more confident in yourself. The jobs that you have to do will be less burdensome because your spirits are not easily deflated.

10
GENERAL SOCIAL PRESSURES

● Identifying blame ● Understanding the teacher's world ● What teachers want from teaching ● What teachers do for students ● Dealing with parents ● Life outside the school

IDENTIFYING BLAME

Teachers often feel themselves to be under a number of pressures from outside the school. Parents are often quoted as a 'pressure' – and equally often as an excuse – and so are public examinations (GCE, CSE, GCSE, etc.) and competition from other schools. Whereas there can be no doubt that external demands can be real and specific for the most part they become generalized as 'pressures'. These outside pressures often arise as an extension of personal anxieties rather than being stressors generated by the school itself. All members of a public profession will be conscious of external demands and it is necessary to distinguish the tangible from the imagined, the real from the false.

Parent demands

Parents often express considerable concern for the way their children are taught but very few parents have precise knowledge about teaching methods; they have only a vague sense of what good teaching is. Because one parent takes an interest in what goes on in the classroom, it does not follow that all the parents of the students in that class will take a critical or informed view.

A teacher needs to distinguish between what one parent is specifically concerned about and what another is. Don't generalize from the interests of one parent and assume that all parents share the same interest.

By and large parents are easily satisfied if a teacher responds positively to their interest and tries to explain clearly what is going on in the classroom. Parents are only occasionally a source of pressure although teachers may feel them to be if they are sensitive to their own classroom practice or trying new methods.

Parents do have a legally valid reason to be interested in what their children do in school and teachers should welcome this interest not resent it. If they do resent it, it is likely to be out of some sense of guilt or anxiety about what they are doing. Guilt does not have to be justified to be felt. When parents are not well-informed, it is a reasonable expectation that teachers should take some pains to explain matters.

Scapegoating of teachers

Teachers sometimes have inflated expectations of society at large. It used to be popular to blame 'society' for the general discomfort felt by many teachers when student behaviour underwent a sea-change in the 1950s. Teachers sometimes see themselves as a major force for social change, as the main upholders of social and moral standards. It is true that for a time after the Second World War there were enormous expectations that all the problems of Britain could be solved through education but gradually a realism set in and now comparatively little is expected − perhaps too little − from the formal system of schooling.

Nevertheless, schools are useful social scapegoats − handy to blame for social wrongs and easy to castigate since all can prove whatever they want by reference to schools. There has always been a good deal of easy rhetoric about schools and teachers themselves have in the past been willing to accept it − at least the favourable bits. One of the social functions of schools is to be the whipping-boys for social discontent; it is one reason they exist for they are at best at surrogate institutions. Other groups are the same − they serve to salve the social conscience − the police, social workers, the medical profession and even the judiciary. Teachers themselves are not exempt from blaming other groups − local councillors and Members of Parliament frequently come in for scholastic lashing.

Teachers are well known for criticizing one another — not specifically, but in general. It helps if teachers support their own profession rather than accepting uninformed attacks from the general public.

Perhaps one of the causes of the sense of general social pressure is the feeling of many teachers that they are preparing students for adult life and the awareness of how difficult and uncertain such a task is. Of course, teachers are not the only ones to be concerned with their students' futures — parents have a closer interest and employers will in due course show a concern. But teachers are agents in that preparation and feel some sense of responsibility. There is very little feedback from the world at large (and the commonest feedback is negative) so teachers never really know how effective they have been.

Some teachers set their sights too high and too unrealistically with the result that they are bound to be dissatisfied with their achievement.

However well a class of students be organized, the ultimate destinations of the pupils will be very varied and no form of preparation for life will suit them all. The teacher's day is excessively busy with detail and minor points of concern and in no way does it relate to the subsequent needs of students in adult life; indeed, many of the preoccupations of the school will be quite different from (even contrary to) the requirements normal adult social life requires.

Perhaps blaming society at large for all the troubles of the school is simply a cry for help that is never heard or never answered.

Teachers tend to be inward-looking in terms of their expectations for their students. The classroom is a small world and what goes on in it is of very little significance when viewed from the world outside. School life is made up of trivia for the most part — as is the daily life of most people at work. Students do not have much of a view of the future; their horizons are quite immediate; they do not look for future satisfactions but present ones; they are only momentarily inspired and for the most part bored.

> If teachers could learn to organize lessons so that they deal with current problems rather than to fulfil distant and idealistic objectives, they could do themselves and their students a better service.

It is a perennial problem that what teachers want to do with their students is too remote. Even the basic subjects are taught in a disconnected way. It is axiomatic that people learn what they have to learn in order to cope with the world as they see it and students who do not learn what the teacher wants them to learn do so simply because they do not need to or see the need to. Teachers cannot face a student with the student's own future however useful it would be if they were able to do so.

Day by day we all learn the arts of survival. The first of student needs is to survive the school day and they may or may not as an additional activity join the teacher in the activities of the day — the learning of lessons.

Employers are mistaken in requiring schools to do what they want. If they want certain skills for their employees, then they must teach them. For the fact is that what employers say they want students to be able to do and what schools can teach may sometimes sound to be the same but in practice are not.

Another reason why teachers may feel under pressure from the demands of the world outside is that they often do not understand it. On the whole most adults do not understand the world outside their own experience either (a truism?) but teachers, for the most part, have less experience of the adult outside world of work than most. Many of the statements teachers make, for instance, about the work place are untrue.

For example, teachers often claim that students will have less freedom at work than they have at school. This is not the general experience of adults in work — or, if they think about it, of teachers themselves since they have more freedom than their own students. They also claim that it is easy to sack someone at work; which as every personnel manager knows is not true. Students can be more easily punished than workers; and there are no student unions that function as trade or professional associations. These may be small examples but they indicate a truth; teachers are no more aware of the realities of the world outside than are their charges, for each of us inhabits our own world.

It is an oddity of the current economic climate that it is popularly thought that teachers are more in need of understanding the industrial world than industrial workers are of schools. Mutual understanding is also necessary because both sides would benefit. It is not just the world of work which holds much that is unknown; many other small worlds exist which will become real to students when they start to earn their living and the values of some of these worlds will be very different from a teacher's imagining — the world of small businesses, the self-employed and the unemployed to mention some of the more obvious ones.

UNDERSTANDING THE TEACHER'S WORLD

Shop talk

Teachers tend to make friends within their own profession. This is true of all professions and not to do so requires an effort of will and determination, but there are certain consequences. One is complacency; talking shop is a favourite pastime of all professions but teachers have a bad press over it. Teachers have the problem that others will join in the conversation and speak with all the authority of their remembered school days; and some will want to get back at teachers for what happened to them at school. Teachers can become very defensive when someone from outside the profession joins in; everyone has some proof and evidence of their criticism (it is generally criticism they join in with) and it often has plausibility.

Teachers can be quick to bridle at criticism especially when most of it is just a whiff of grapeshot across the bows — too general to be answered but too irritatingly true to be ignored.

It becomes a source of stress to be assailed continually by 'outsiders' with criticism of the profession when you are trying to do your best but know only too well that a lot more needs to be done.

One suspects that teachers find the general lack of sympathy with them just a bit too much to take at times. Many people draw on their own experience of school as if it were only yesterday; few people recognize that schools have changed — and teachers themselves sometimes wonder if they have.

An interesting characteristic of shop talk is that though it may have a common theme the talkers are often at cross-purposes. Young parents with babies constantly talk past one another, not entering into a dialogue but sequencing monologues in a ritual of talking about their offspring. Teachers can be like this, taking it in turns to say their piece but unrelated to what anyone else says. Talking like this without connecting is common enough but it may sometimes be a symptom of anxiety and emotional discomfort.

Teachers sometimes assume that even the strangers they engage in conversation actually understand the intricacies of their school and enter on long monologues about their day at school, a sign no doubt that teachers do not have the right sort of opportunity to talk their concerns through where they ought to, with an understanding colleague at school.

Often, teachers assume too much understanding on the part of outsiders, including parents, and press on with detailed accounts of their work and concerns. Teachers often seem to have a proprietary interest in their work and can slip from the specific to the general with disconcerting ease. They seem to find it easy to talk about individual children but not so easy to talk about educational issues though they can rapidly generalize from a case of one.

There is also a tendency (not confined to teachers but not uncharacteristic of them) to pontificate and hold opinions that can be disconcerting to more cautious adults. Perhaps this is to stereotype teachers but then non-teachers find it easy to stereotype teachers and to have their stereotyping confirmed. There often seems to be a general lack of sympathy for teachers which they can find very worrying. Yet as in many other professions, teachers seem to work quite hard at perpetuating the public myths about themselves rather than trying to dispel them.

Teachers and families

Because teachers spend their time habitually working with children or young people in a dependency creating situation, they often bring away from the classroom many of their attitudes towards students and direct them towards their families and friends. Children and spouses of teachers (especially head teachers) often complain that they are treated at home like pupils. This is not always true but it is difficult for anyone to behave in quite distinct ways to people who are close to them.

While this may also be true of other professional groups such as clergymen and social workers, with teachers there is often a different sense of authority that has little to do with expertise and more with the need to be in charge. Teachers often feel hurt when their offspring accuse them of being 'teachy' or when friends say they are being bossy but attitudes and behaviour patterns learned in the job are hard to change.

The situation is made worse by the historical expectations of teachers. There is much folklore about teachers and schools which includes the idea of teacher as policeman and upholder of moral standards. Teachers have been given their right to punish to an extent allowed only to prison officers, ship's captains and masters of workhouses and asylums. Children used to be threatened with the policeman or the teacher if they misbehaved and teachers still have the right to punish outside the law. Fortunately the practice is for most part of the past but the mythology still lingers.

There is a strange phenomenon that some people actually claim to have benefited by or even enjoyed being punished by teachers, and to have welcomed especially corporal punishment – that special perversion of the English psyche. Obviously some teachers enjoy administering punishments since they do it so much. It is often said that 'my best teachers were the strictest' as if that were virtuous on both sides. Then there is the fatuous 'It never did me any harm . . .'.

Clearly there is an ambiguous message being given to teachers by members of the public at large. On the one hand they are being told they ought to be more strict and disciplining, while on the other they are told they are too authoritarian and need to respect students more. Most teachers would tend towards the latter view but they are aware that parents, etc. expect them to do in a disagreeable way what they cannot do for their children at home. Such uncertainty about expectations is a likely cause of stress particularly when dealing with difficult students.

Awakening of industrial attitudes

Unexpectedly teachers have found themselves overturning most of their espoused values to engage in an industrial dispute which had nothing to do with the kind of relationships schools declare to exist within themselves. That much of the political activity was inept was a consequence of inexperience in confrontation but it made very clear the stark difference between the educational world and the larger world outside. Many teachers did not like what happened but support for industrial action was almost universal.

The recent period of industrial unrest in British education has exposed the fragility of the norms and values of the school when teachers are tested publicly in the tough world of economic reality.

Teachers sometimes behaved in ways that would have received extreme reprimand had they been used by students in school and on some occasions teachers in public set no better an example than other adults engaged in political and industrial action.

Schools need to examine more closely the value system on which they actually function and to note the differences between teacher behaviour and pupil behaviour with regard to school values. In some ways schools are very confusing to members as well as outsiders because the rhetoric obscures the practice.

For example, there are contradictions in what schools declare to be the nature of relations between students and teachers. On the one hand schools stress the need for co-operation as a *sine qua non* of school relationships among pupils but they reward success in competitive activities. This is an old contradiction but a serious one because an organization cannot value equally competiveness which must include individuality, self-interest and entrepreneurship and also claim to foster conformity, collective reponsibility and obedience. Teachers just do not recognize fully enough the confused values they demonstrate to students for they appear arbitrary in what they praise and what they punish.

WHAT TEACHERS WANT FROM TEACHING

Rewards and status

The status of teachers in society is generally considered to have declined over the years. If teachers believe themselves to be less well rewarded than other 'comparable' members of society they will be resentful; long holidays do not count against the company car. Part of this sense of being less well-rewarded comes from the kind of relationship teachers have with their 'clients'. Students tend when very young to have little thought of saying 'Thank you' and when they are older they tend at best to take teachers for granted and at worst to despise them.

It is not surprising that teachers should have a high level of discontent simply because the direct rewards are so few. It may well be that much teacher discontent is talk rather than reality because there is also some evidence that teachers as a whole have a high level of satisfaction in their job even if the circumstances around teaching leave something to be desired.

In any case, the educational service is ambivalent over what it rewards. While it will usually be claimed that it is 'good teaching' that really counts it would be difficult to prove this by reference to the rewards system. Promotion seems to be given for anything but good teaching and the system tends to undermine the stability of a good teaching service by encouraging teachers to move schools for promotion.

Extrovert teachers

Most teachers are probably extroverts and enjoy the interpersonal relations part of their job best (that is, they enjoy working with people rather than on their own) so they need a lot of good feedback from their students.

But extroverts are prone to depression, sometimes in extreme forms, when the necessary stimuli are not forthcoming. This means the vacations may be more stressful than the term time for some teachers. They may also need variety and sometimes schools do not have enough variety in them to stimulate teachers — despite the fact that teachers usually claim variety to be a welcome characteristic of their job. Some teachers may well become bored more often than they will admit and it may be that for many, out-of-school activities are an important aspect of the job, since it is an area where the teacher can quickly influence the direction activities take.

Primary schools may offer more immediate challenges to teachers who need stimulation because the children have so much energy. But in secondary schools student energy is usually strongly repressed so teachers are not stimulated any more than are their pupils. The general level of largely purposeless activity in secondary schools demands a lot of energy from teachers simply to keep students engaged and must in itself be a de-energizing experience

Unrealistic sense of importance

Teachers may believe their job to be more important than other people consider it; they probably claim too much for them and education in general. Teachers have elevated the idea of public examinations to a high place in the public consciousness from which they can with difficulty displace it. Examinations are not really very important in the general scheme of life but the school system has made them as if they were the very essence of life. Apparently anyone with 'poor' results in GCE is really a failure; everything that is said to deny that fails to convince.

WHAT TEACHERS DO FOR STUDENTS

The insistence on qualifications even rebounds on the profession itself so that now all teachers must have a university degree. Teachers also value themselves in terms of where they obtained their degree – college, polytechnic or university in ascending order of esteem. Some teachers feel the need to expiate the disgrace of a poor degree and study for a second degree in their own time. Many see the need for a further degree, diploma or professional qualification as a necessary requirement for promotion.

> Teaching is a profession caught up in many of the negative dimensions of its own value system. Teachers worry a good deal about being competent enough or adequately qualified, and some of them feel they have not quite made the grade.

Evaluation of achievement

The use of national (i.e. public) examinations as the key measure of school attainment is a yardstick of comparison to the classroom which ought not to be there. Instead of children being valued for their own sakes and their own achievement, the effect of using national criteria is to undervalue the achievement of most students and also of most of their teachers.

Teachers will explain to parents where their child is in relation to national achievement. ('He will do quite well in 5C. He is not GCE standard but with a bit of hard work – and you might be able to help him here – he should get about 3 CSEs.') A teacher with a class of clever students will do well by national criteria; but how do you feel when you have a 'poor' fifth form that can be predicted to get 'poor' results?

> Is the only significant measure of a secondary-school teacher's achievement to be found in public examination results? Much professional recognition depends on 'getting good exam results', which seems a very unfair way of evaluating a teacher's work.

Schools are supposed to be achievement orientated but also to concentrate on the individual; they must be multi-ethnic yet respect individual

religious beliefs; they must provide for special needs yet not favour
children unfairly; they should use public examinations yet also provide
individual profiles of progress; they must give social and moral education
yet not political education; they must give sex education and not offend
any minority; they must fit young people for employment yet also prepare
them for life where they may be unemployed; they must teach science
and mathematics to all; they must teach music and the arts to all; every
child should speak a foreign language; all children should be highly
literate so presumably they will all read *The Times, Guardian* or *Independent*; they must learn basic skills but not waste time on cookery, car
mechanics, gardening, or going on trips; they must develop their individual
talents but be constrained by a core curriculum.

> It is not the students who suffer so much from the basic contradictions
> but the teachers who can only develop a form of schizophrenia to be
> able to tolerate and even perpetuate them.

Process not content of learning

To cope more successfully in the classroom, teachers must be more
realistic about what actually happens and what is achievable for themselves
in their personal terms and for their students in theirs. Teachers may
mistakenly aim at 'the education of the whole child', which is a practical
impossibility even within a large and richly resourced school. Much more
modest aims should be conceived that have short-term relevance. It is
important to have clear expectations of students and to look for the
fulfilment of their needs not the teacher's ambitions. Such objectives as
getting through the syllabus at any cost just will not do for either student
or teacher satisfaction. In education it is never the content that matters so
much as the process that eventually embraces the content.

Very often the dialogue teachers and parents have together is confused
and not seldom at cross-purposes. Teachers, like any other worker, use a
jargon all their own, which they usually fail to acknowledge. (Just what
does, 'average' or 'doing well' or 'not very attentive' mean?) School
culture is exceedingly complex and the words teachers use are often
enigmatic to parents and others outside the school. Even when parents
understand the words ('Josy is in Set Three for Communication Studies
but Set Five for Keyboard Skills') they may not understand the context

and frame of reference' Parents must often seem mildly stupid to teachers when they look blank or mutter platitudes.

Teachers must appear very daunting when they speak with certitude about educational abstractions. Teachers are easily threatened by parents' questions because they often do not understand their provenance. A parent who is simply seeking information may appear aggressive ('Why cannot Deidre sit with her friend Anita in Home Economics? I think she's wasting her time doing flower arrangements'). Another may simply be exercising what would to them be a normal right even though it may go against what a teacher would want ('I don't want Wayne to come to school next Friday because his grandparents are coming. I don't think gym does him any good').

Occasionally, teachers will transfer their feelings about a student to the parents with what may be dire results — such as treating the parents with the same defensiveness as the student. Parents and teachers live in different social and organizational worlds and yet there is a general assumption (on all sides) that schools are an open world. Outsiders to each school — and that includes teachers from other schools — are not privy to the cultural undertones and niceties and will frequently guess them wrong.

DEALING WITH PARENTS

Teacher expectations of parents

Teachers create many of their own problems when dealing with parents because of the disposition they have towards them. Teachers' attitudes to parents are often ambivalent and may include 'intolerance' and suspicion. Teachers, particularly at secondary level, may be latently hostile to parents and sometimes jealous. Teachers expect both too much of parents and not enough and may misjudge the real interest and support that parents offer.

On the one hand parents may be accepted as being co-partners in supporting their children's learning but on the other hand they may be seen as not always giving the support to teachers that they need. Teachers may see themselves as the experts in the education of children and parents as the amateurs, not always to be trusted even to help with their children's reading.

> In some ways parents and teachers are rivals for the affection and
> loyalty of the pupil.

Parents at parents' evenings often feel at a disadvantage and are seldom
able to indulge in the straightforward questioning they would adopt in
other situations such as at the bank or garden centre. Teachers and
parents often 'talk past' one another because much of what goes on in
schools is not properly understood by parents and teachers see no need to
explain everything. Teachers seldom have enough time to talk with parents
and to put them at their ease, for many parents will experience a return
of many of their own feelings about being a pupil when they visit the
school.

> Schools should try to make the reception of parents as unlike the
> memories of their own school days as possible. If parents are put at
> their ease they will be less likely to be overcritical and defensive.

Teachers sometimes adopt a parental tone or attitude towards parents,
treating them as if they were children rather than other adults. They can
be very controlling of parents in a meeting, however welcoming and
warm they may be at the outset.

> Why is the assumption so often made the teachers should be the
> dominant side in a parental interview? Who is really interviewing
> whom?

It is usually assumed that explanations from the teacher will be adequate
for parental questions but it is a false assumption; parents may ask good
questions which teachers answer badly. There may be a tendency for
teachers to see themselves as better parents than other parents and think
they know better how to bring up children — certainly in some cases this
will be true but not in all.

It is worth an attempt to reframe the teacher's view of parents and the
family by trying to reverse the way the relationship is viewed; the parents
could be viewed as the experts and the more knowledgeable and the
teacher as the one who needs information and advice.

Social differences between teachers and parents

Social class differences (or whatever terminology one uses to describe social structure) are always likely to create problems of communication since there may be a lack of understanding or appreciation of each other's viewpoint. For example, it may be very difficult for a family with five children and a limited income to arrange a quiet place which is warm enough for a child to do his or her homework and yet many children are penalized for work which is a direct consequence of home conditions.

Many 'working-class' parents are unlikely to have enjoyed their days at school and will have felt uncomfortable in an alien social climate. Many of these parents will have a history of unpleasant experiences with teachers and will find it very hard indeed to relate to them. When they meet teachers in any circumstances they will feel inferior or aggressive and lacking in confidence. If they visit teachers at their own former school they will be even more intimidated.

Sometimes parents are invited to attend school to discuss their child – or even peremptorily 'sent for' – and this can be a most chilling experience for adults whose memories of schooldays are not of the warmest. Many adults, whatever their background and upbringing, will not have the particular social skills for coping will teachers and especially head teachers.

In all of these situations, teachers can make significant inroads towards facilitating more positive encounters by thinking through what the objectives are in all of the situations and in terms of putting themselves in the parents' shoes. From the teacher's position it is important to understand what is going on with parents if encounters are not to be stressful to either party. If parents feel stressed when meeting teachers, teachers will feel stressed in dealing with the situation unless they have very specific skills for coping.

If parents arrive at school looking for trouble, teachers have to know how to defuse the situation, calm down the parents and enter into a meaningful dialogue. This cannot be done if parents are undervalued, or used as surrogates for dealing with obstreperous students. That is why teachers need to understand how the years have built up a mythology of parents that brings with it serious problems for teachers in their relations with not only the general public but the parents of their students.

Standing and status of parents

Teachers could begin an evaluation of the relationship with parents in terms of the kind of information they give and the way in which it is given. For one thing, it is counter-productive for a teacher to pretend to making. Parents and teachers both are parts of the problem. But the as being condenscending.

School handbooks need to be prepared very carefully not to convey the wrong tone; some of them are a confused mixture of styles and values because sections have been written by different teachers. The information must be aimed at the understanding of the reader, and not be a product of internal and private concerns. Such questions as the kind of access available must be made clear and it should reflect a concern for the convenience of the parent not the convenience of the school. It is worth reflecting on hospital visiting hours and the impact they have on relatives and friends; hospitals have moved towards more flexible hours in the interests of patients and relatives not of the organization of ward tasks.

It is worth recalling how many people deal with unsolicited corres-pondence when general communications are sent from the school. It is quite usual for most circular or even personal communications from official bodies to be ignored, at least for a considerable time. Some people are even afraid of official communications and try to leave them unread.

Parents may relate to the school as they will to other official institutions and teachers should not expect special treatment for they will certainly be disappointed.

Parents' evenings

Talking about individual pupils on parents' evening, etc. can be a most uncomfortable experience for both parents and teachers. Teachers find parents' faces blurring as they struggle to remember whose child is theirs. They are conscious of a queue of parents and too little time to speak fully enough to them all.

Parents may see themselves being herded around as if they were senior pupils, made to wait in queues as if they were at the post office, and then having a five-minute talk to someone who is not at all like the description given by their child and whose nickname has been confused with the real name. Finding something meaningful to talk about after the first pleasantries and raw information has been passed on is impossible unless there are only a few students in the 'set' and plenty of time. It is usually impossible for the parent to fit the information about one child into context without knowing a lot about other children in the same class; except in exceptional circumstances the parent will know only one or two of their child's friends.

> Schools should experiment with different ways of working with parents that involve more face-to-face contact between parents and students and a wide range of informal situations where parents can meet teachers and one another even if many parents only manage a few visits to such events.

It seems strange that parents should have so limited and cursory acquaintance with the school, normally visiting it only on some serious or critical occasion. Why cannot parents and other adults be a much more integrated part of the school than they are? Is there really the need to keep parents away from both teachers and students that lies behind the organizational assumptions of most schools?

The child in the middle

Many teachers are in one way or another apprehensive about parents. For one thing, they know that students will have told their parents something about them and such information will be distorted by virtue of the position the student is in. But also teachers have a personal relationship with each student that is private; it does not belong to the parent and yet it is of consequence to them. Confidences built up between student and teacher are no longer to be held confidential because the parent has the right to know.

Teachers sometimes feel they have an understanding with a student that is 'better' than the understanding of the parents. Parents may feel the obverse of this. They and their child have an intimate relationship which the teacher has no right to be part of and yet, under the right circumstances, may need to be party to. Parents and teachers eye one another with circumspection both wanting to protect the student yet also wanting to betray them; wanting to preserve confidences yet knowing they might have to be shared. Many teachers are more protective towards their students when parents are around than they may wish to acknowledge.

In the end, the key to relating to parents is the same as for relating to other adults: courtesy, respect and an appreciation of a point of view. To solve problems between two parties there must be an equality of sharing and an equal willingness to seek mutually acceptable solutions. Teachers cannot deliver ultimatums or demand that only their interpretation of a situation should be allowed. A school should not call parents in to tell them what will be done; there must be full and open discussion about ways and means.

Students are often in the middle of a situation that is not of their own making. Parents and teachers both are parts of the problem. But the school's part will also be largely of the school's own creation while the parents' part as well will be largely of theirs. There are three problems to be solved not one. The most neglected problem will often be the child's because no one will want to take much trouble trying to find out how the child experiences his or her problem.

LIFE OUTSIDE THE SCHOOL

Signs of being a teacher

Teachers may have problems in their life away from school. For example, how can a teacher stop being a teacher when at home, in the garden or at the sports club? It is claimed by many people that they can always spot a teacher on holiday because they make everything into an educational visit. Others claim they can always tell teachers by their clothes. Yet others by the way they cannot control their children.

It is unlikely that this is any more true of teachers than other professional groups but such views are part of the way teachers are perceived by others. But sometimes teachers go on at length about teaching and schools and parents, so it is worth trying to avoid conversations about teaching unless the others really are well-informed.

If you want to save yourself from getting into a discussion that may make you feel uncomfortable:

Never talk about what goes on at work.
Never rise to the bait that almost anyone who learns that you are a teacher will offer.

Perhaps the social group that can provide the greatest real support for a teacher is their own family. On the whole members of the families cope with one another very well and are not very impressed by self-opinionation and pomposity; they can also be remarkably supportive when you are feeling down. A well-adjusted family life allows you to be so nearly yourself as to make no difference, allowing you to make excursions into other specialist groups where your special needs are catered for.

In the family we have to know our place for we will not be indulged unnecessarily. Other support groups reinforce family support by giving appropriate feedback in ways we can easily deal with, however hard the comment might be; they combine to give us a realistic sense of worth and regard. We should all work hard at building a good family life and have at least one other support group outside our work place.

Getting out of a rut

Sometimes we feel in a rut and fed up in spite of having a range of interests and activities. When this happens we need the company of friends who are likely to open up to us new possibilities or to enliven ones that have become stale. We need to have enough variety in our interests to counteract the tedium of work. If we find that all our time is taken up with school we must deliberately find time to do other and quite different things. Sometimes the effort is enough to break the boredom without actually becoming committed to joining an organization.

> The secret of getting out of lethargy is just to do anything so long as it makes you change your pattern, however briefly. Simply acknowledging that you need to do something is the first step towards doing it.

The richer our life outside, the more our school life will be enriched. An important effect of being involved in other forms of activity is that it changes the way we look at our work, puts everything into a new relationship and points up the triviality with which we have become obsessed.

Although teachers claim that they work much beyond school hours they nevertheless have more freedom to organize their time as they wish. They can do things over the holiday periods that most other people cannot do. It is worth turning this time to advantage. Some may go on long holidays or visit foreign parts not just as holiday-makers but on some enterprise or project. Some go on exchanges with other teachers from overseas by taking advantage of different national vacation patterns. Some are engaged in social work of one sort or another and some are able to go on school trips in addition to their own holidays; you cannot go on a school trip without trying out new ways of relating to people. Time is at the disposal of teachers in a way it is not for most other workers and finding ways to exploit this resource is a major element in personal development. The more you can be away from school the better your coping will be with the job when you are there.

11
HEAD TEACHERS: A SPECIAL CASE

- Problems of understanding the role • Why heads can be lonely
- Choosing a stance • Problems of professional skills • Leadership
skills • Managerial distancing • Relationships outside the school
- Being yourself and sustaining yourself

PROBLEMS OF UNDERSTANDING THE ROLE

Head teachers hold a particular position in the organization of the school that is quite unlike the top job in any other organization. Titles tell you very little about the nature of the organization but head teachers are familiar figures from everyone's past and appear to be something special. By and large, head teachers are held to be responsible for just about everything that goes on in a school and are thought of as having a ubiquitous presence. Schools encourage this belief and some heads seem to rejoice in it. Some heads will claim that they need to know everything that goes on in their school and will ensure they are kept informed in some systematic way. Some will want to vet all visitors either through their secretary, through a reception system or by ensuring that their room is by the main entrance of the school.

By and large, heads are the only members of school staff to have a decent room for their own exclusive use and it is usually strategically placed at the centre of the administrative system both physically and ideologically. It will possibly be the only room where visitors can be met and entertained in any comfort. A consequence is that the head is under some pressure as host on behalf of the school.

Role confusion

The term *head teacher* implies that heads are primarily teachers, but it does not have to mean that they are teachers as well as bosses. However, there is here a dilemma for many heads — choosing between being a teacher and being a manager. Of course, in some schools there is no option about teaching; in small schools a head will be counted as a teaching member and even in some secondary schools will have been appointed in the expectation that teaching is part of the job. This expectation does nothing to resolve the dilemma for the fact is it is not possible to be both top person and an ordinary member of the organization. Even among heads themselves there is some confusion because heads often speak of themselves as 'captain of the ship' without realizing that captains are not ratings and a ship would not get far out to sea if they were. Captains do a different job from other sailors.

So a head's first problem is to do with uncertainty about what they want to be. Many continue to want the best of both worlds which is a recipe for disaster by all normal standards. Presumably heads take the post because they want to be in a more powerful and influential position than that of a class teacher. Obviously, if they preferred the classroom and the subordinate position they would have stayed there. This is as good a reason as any for seeking promotion.

Many heads will admit to wanting to become heads because they felt that the heads they worked under were inadequate or that they themselves could do the job just as well (and promotion would mean more money). There is no doubt that being a head offers much more personal freedom than being in any other position in the school, considered over all. The position also brings with it a number of opportunities that are not available to other teachers. Not many people entering a school for the first time as head have many pangs of regret about not having a conventional school timetable.

It may well be that teaching is an important part of a head's personal image and one they are reluctant to give up. There are plenty of opportunities for teaching if you run the school and you can pick and choose who you want to teach. But it is possible to do more than teaching because the whole curriculum comes into your hands when you take over a school and the satisfactions of the wider field will almost certainly be valued against those of the narrower ones. After all, a head can always go back to teaching as a class teacher but the choice of becoming a head was presumably taken with some hopes and expectations that were larger than the view of the classroom.

Where heads seem to miss out is in the close relationships that are often experienced by teachers in the camaraderie of the staff common room.

Heads as managers

There is a great deal of circumstantial evidence that heads find it very difficult to think of themselves as managers, especially strategic managers. Managing the classroom is not the same as managing the school; it is of quite a different order and quality. Sadly, head-teacher training in management skills is still very much in its infancy. There is quite inadequate preparation for headship and no coherent pattern of training and development once a head is in the job. This makes heads quite vulnerable and sometimes they react by blustering shows of overconfidence.

There has, however, been a considerable change over the last ten years in heads' attitudes to 'industrial' management training methods. At one time they claimed that schools were quite unlike industry but now the current theme seems to be that schools have a lot to learn. This has led to an increased confidence and a greater sense of reality about the job. Heads are taking the idea of themselves as managers much more seriously.

Another distinction needs to be made if we are to clear up the confusion over roles and the self-concept that relates to them. There is a difference between 'administration' and 'management' and if the distinction is not made in practice a great deal of personal and organizational confusion ensues.

Expressed simply, the distinction is that administration is concerned with routine activities while management is concerned with strategies. Both involve working with people (personal and industrial relations) though management requires it at a much deeper level but otherwise they present the head with two totally different standpoints.

It is more than likely that most heads wanted to be heads so they could become managers and not administrators. It is also more than likely that most heads find themselves trying to be administrators and not managers.

For most heads the critical decision which will affect their attitude to their job and determine how they cope with it will be deciding to be a manager and to develop the skills and attitudes that are appropriate. This being so, they will have to make critical decisions about the administration of the school which does not lead to a conflict of interests and people.

WHY HEADS CAN BE LONELY

Isolation and headship

One of the hurtful effects of taking the top position but not knowing how to fill it in managerial terms is that no one really knows how to relate to the head; it is especially confusing to the deputies. There is much talk about the 'senior management team' in secondary education and team work in primary schools but without a clear understanding of where the head stands in the team, the development of truly collective activity is impossible and the head becomes increasingly isolated organizationally and emotionally from colleagues.

In most schools deputies are held in mixed regard. Some are seen to be of head-teacher potential, others as having reached their highest level, and not a few as aberrations of the system. (Education seems to be as good as any other kind of organization in managing to get a significant number of people in the wrong position and then being unable to do anything about them; and in teaching promotion is not often a possible solution.) In many schools the position of deputy is organizationally uncertain; that is, there is even more uncertainty over whether deputies are teachers or managers and in most cases the teacher option is chosen with the consequence that the head is even more isolated than ever.

It has always been one of the most popular complaints among heads that they are isolated. It is claimed that they are made to stand apart from their colleagues with no one to confide in, carrying the whole burden of the school and being the bulwark against enraged parents and the public and the cushion between 'the office' and their colleagues. There is no doubt that some heads see themselves in this way and have suffered the consequences.

> The way some heads isolate themselves from their colleagues must be one of the biggest contributing factors to stress and unhappiness that heads encounter. Yet it is entirely of their own making because it is not a situation inherent in organization but rather a function of the management style of the heads themselves.

In every organization it is possible to develop teams of people who provide full emotional support as well as functional support (i.e. in carrying out the various jobs of the organization). Some closeness and friendship with other members in the school is a prerequisite for survival at every level; it is not enough, as many heads do, to go outside for support and encouragement only from other heads.

The senior management team and other functional teams must be developed in a spirit of co-operation, mutuality, equality of regard and a recognition that each member is at the same managerial level. The mistake in many schools is that hierarchic distinctions are made too finely; perhaps the salary scales contribute to that.

Schools are too conscious of people's ages for their own good probably because they are obsessed with the ages of students. Just as children are moved up with each year of age so teachers are moved up as they get older. Departments in secondary schools seem to place everyone in a rank order of some sort. Heads may perceive their colleagues in much the same way as they perceive the students, only their colleagues are an extended sixth form.

Some heads have great difficulty in accepting even their senior colleagues as equals but if they do not they have a problem of their standing with them. Perhaps that is why many heads tend to be paternalistic towards their colleagues or even patronizing; some are even authoritarian and teachers habitually refer to heads as autocratic. So much so that it is part of the folklore of schooling that heads see themselves as above everyone else and often treat teachers and even parents as if they were pupils.

Of course, many teachers collude with this demeaning attitude, refusing to see themselves as professional equals. It can be very frustrating for a head who really does want to deal with his or her colleagues as adult professionals to find them developing subordinate attitudes and behaviour. For one thing, it is difficult to trust people who do not trust themselves.

Perhaps the easiest way of presenting the problems of headship which many heads undoubtedly create for themselves is to suggest that they may be taking themselves too seriously and are perhaps sometimes prone to the failing of pomposity or even arrogance to cover up their own sense of uncertainty and inadequacy. If bosses cannot define their jobs clearly enough for themselves no one else will but the effect will be to incapacitate them before they begin.

CHOOSING A STANCE

Knowing quite clearly what managerial behaviour is (or administrative behaviour if that is the choice) and acting in the appropriate ways will lead to a much greater sense of satisfaction and achievement. Above all, it will enable other members of the school to define their own jobs and let them get on with them without undue interference. On the whole, heads seem to have a low level of trust in their colleagues, partly for fear of the consequences and partly through anxiety in being so universally responsible.

Trust depends on the ability to continue to accept people who fail or let you down; if you never allow anyone to fail you will never be able to trust them.

Proprietary interest

Heads sometimes appear to have a proprietary interest in the school. When heads say 'My school' they may well think of it in that possessive way; at least, teachers often comment as such. Most other members of a school refer to it as 'our' school, identifying with other members. Certainly heads are in danger of becoming too attached to a school as if they were the main stakeholder and this has several stress-including consequences.

For one, it encourages the head to feel more responsibility for things that go wrong than is appropriate. For another, it means that vision is circumscribed to what the head perceives or wants and this is potentially a creator of conflict with others who have a different vision. It also means the head is likely to fill a more corrective role than promotional one, and the conflicts here include adverse feedback. It means that the head will increasingly distance him- or herself (and become distanced as a consequence of colleagues' response) and will reduce the amount of positive feedback from colleagues so increasing their isolation. It may alienate staff who feel excluded and/or patronized. It means such heads believe their perceptions of reality in the school are clearer than anyone else's.

Proprietorial heads have to carry a burden of responsibility entirely of their own making since no one else will accept the importance such heads place on themselves.

Being over-identified with school means that the fortunes of the school and those of the head are intertwined in such way that the head will be hurt by any changes. By adopting a managerial stance, however, the head can observe the school objectively and in turn protected from the emotional stress of identification.

PROBLEMS OF PROFESSIONAL SKILLS

Lack of training

The transition from classroom to headship is a sudden one even when the previous position was that of deputy head. Because there is no managerial tradition in schooling, heads do not have the experience necessary before promotion and must learn a whole set of new skills very quickly. It is not just the skills that have to be learned it is an appreciation of the context in which they have to be applied because suddenly the head is closer to the external pressures on the school than they have ever been.

The fact is that very few people in schools other than heads have to face up to their public on their own. In most other organizations many more people have to deal with customers or clients than schools do. Because schools treat students as secondary clients not primary ones, they always look over their shoulder to the parent or LEA or employer or whatever.

The variety of skills required of heads in their capacity of head is greater than would normally be required of any other manager. School heads are expected to be works manager (*pace* the school caretaker), general manager (*pace* the senior deputy), chairperson of the board (even when the chairperson of governors is active on the school's behalf), advertising manager, research manager and personnel manager and goodness knows what else. The way most schools are organized means no one can fill any of these functions adequately and it is unfortunate that many heads feel they have to do so instead of organizing their deputies and senior colleagues to fill these staff functions. In managerial terms schools do badly on staff (support) functions even if they do reasonably on line functions (i.e. teaching).

The importance of respect

The one skill a head can be expected to have by virtue of experience is that of teacher and facilitator and yet this is probably the one skill least used in management. A good teacher can manage the learning of a class of over thirty students and motivate them to take responsibility for their own learning. This area of skills is not essentially any different from that required to manage teaching staff. Of course, if heads behave as a traditional teacher towards their colleagues they will be in trouble (and some heads undoubtedly are) but if they regard their best teaching and facilitator skills as the essential management skills there should be no contradiction and no condescension.

If a head cannot regard his or her colleagues as professional equals it is important to reflect why and to find ways of changing the situation. For some heads there is a residual resentment of colleagues which may well be the result of a guilt feeling about themselves. Not all teachers respect themselves as teachers or even persons. The point at issue is the nature of the working relationship between head and colleagues. If the work of school management is really to be shared among the most able members of staff and not become an unnecessary burden on the head it will be necessary to admit that colleagues may know better how to do things than the head. A wise head will be glad that that is so.

Personally generated pressures

The need to feel in complete control at all times is one of the stresses that many heads generate for themselves. There really is no need to know everything that is going on and what everyone is doing and if colleagues are trusted there is no problem about not knowing. Some heads do feel personally vulnerable to criticism of the school especially when that criticism scapegoats the head personally. One reason the general public focuses on the head is that schools do not present a variety of alternative 'targets'. If heads set themselves up to draw the fire from the public then they will certainly get hurt.

There are ways in which the school can have a public presence which do not centre on a single individual. For example, schools with a brass band that engages in local competitions and festivals soon becomes an alternative symbol to the school itself. Where schools work as part of the community instead of apart from local social life, other people become involved in school activity and the school is not symbolically isolated.

Some heads wish to control the wrong things. It is necessary to be more selective about the responsibilities undertaken and more encouraging of colleagues to accept full responsibility for an area of activity. The details of the curriculum can be left to teachers − it is claimed that one of the benefits of TVEI is that most heads know nothing about the content and so have to confine themselves to managing the margins. There should be a lot more of managing at the margins by the head and a determination to do only what no one else can reasonably be expected to do.

Lack of delegation

Heads can do silly things in terms of work loads such as reading and signing all reports, interviewing all students who are going into the sixth form, attending all school events even if it means attending the school play six times, checking on lunch-time supervision, and a myriad of jobs that outsiders would consider trivial and not appropriate for a head. There are heads who would die before relinquishing one of these cherished tasks claiming that they are at the very core of a caring headship.

It would be difficult to find any single task which all heads feel essential and indeed which all heads perform. One aspect, however, does characterize the daily work load of most heads – trivia. Often, it has to be admitted, necessary trivia but trivia nevertheless. More than anything, heads need to look carefully at how they organize their time. For most heads, inviting a colleague or management consultant to give advice would save a great deal of anxiety and overwork.

Coping mechanisms for heads

Heads have one advantage over their school colleagues so far as coping with stress is concerned. They can more easily find a bolt hole. This alone makes it difficult to sympathize too readily with heads when they talk of being stressed. There are any number of devices for avoiding stress and indeed for coping with stress. The commonest (which is well-known within the profession) is involvement in union affairs. Anything that takes the head out of school with some regularity is likely to be either a stress-coping mechanism or a consequence of stress; there is after all no reason why anyone should want to leave school except on essential school business. For example, attendance at Rotary Club may or may not be 'necessary' but it is not compulsory and involves a choice on the part of a head. Whether this choice is made in the interests of the school or for personal reasons is a matter of some importance.

One frustration that heads may have is wanting to teach more and feeling that their professional standing with colleagues depends more on their teaching skills than their management abilities. This will be particularly so if they are unsure of themselves as managers and of their managerial skills – especially if they are not very sure what the necessary management skills are. A pressure that heads often feel is to prove competence (in whatever you like) and the fear of not being competent is often very real to them.

When they meet together, it is not at all easy to ask for help so heads do not naturally find the kind of support among their peers that they need. Indeed, the reverse is often the case. Heads tend to collude with one another in not facing up to professional and personal problems and to ascribe the difficulties in running schools to other sources — poor deputies, incompetent teachers, inadequate resourcing, unrealistic demands from local authorities, and so on. Yet no one expects heads to be perfect except themselves.

Self-esteem

It may well be that the large number of young people in schools is a factor in making it difficult for teachers to experience an adequate range of relationships with adults. Most of the contact that heads have with teachers is in a relationship when someone else is being discussed; that is, it is less a relationship with the teacher than a brief 'case conference' over students. This means that heads and teachers do not engage in real one-to-one adult relationships but have their own relationships distorted by the relationship with the student.

Schools spend a lot of time dealing with pupil problems and issues that may not be matched by enough time on teacher relationships. In any case, students are often used as intermediaries in relationships between teachers; sometimes quite severe controversies are fought out with students as pawns. In many issues that are really between heads and teachers students are used as go-betweens or surrogates. Heads could usefully give attention to the true nature of their relationships with colleagues.

Heads are reasonably independent of their local authorities though the situation varies from place to place. The general tenor of conversation among heads is that they feel autonomous and able to run their schools much as they want to. But the positive support they receive from their LEAs varies and some are without the close emotional support they need, being left too much on their own. There is a subtle dividing line between support and interference but it is easy to interpret intended support as interference if one is not feeling too secure.

Everyone expects a great deal of heads — probably too much by any reckoning — and the demands considerably exceed the praise, so it is easy to become defensive and in so doing perceive even help as implying criticism. When anyone feels particularly bad about performance it is very difficult to recognize even praise let alone straightforward comment. Some people create for themselves a hostile world in which most encounters become criticism. It is easy for heads to become oversensitive (even paranoid) and once this happens there is a tendency to see confirmation of things being wrong rather than support for things going well.

LEADERSHIP SKILLS

Value conflicts

When an individual is in charge of an organization, there is a tendency to ascribe personal values to the institution and assume that other members hold to the same value system. The problem for schools is that while there are undoubtedly operational values the values of people in the system may be at variance. All parents do not share the same values and some of them will be in conflict. If one adds to this the personal values of the head and the assumption that the head's values are the dominant ones there cannot but be problems. The big danger for heads is in overvaluing their own importance just because they hold a top position. Some heads undoubtedly have delusions of grandeur and it would seem that some of the 'great' heads of the past were smitten with a high level of conceit but in these days, the cult of 'great men' is not fashionable and people would rather put heads down than overpraise them.

Heads and leadership

Heads are, of course, formal or nominal leaders simply by virtue of being titular head of their institution. At one time, it was believed that leadership was a matter of an individual possessing the appropriate traits – for example, being wise, experienced, forthright, determined, strong-minded, dedicated and so on. Leadership theories no longer express this view but portray leadership as being more contingent on the needs of the situation, perhaps the right person for the right job. It is even more likely that leadership does not lie with one individual and is certainly not an attribute that comes with the job.

Leadership is in fact a function of the organization; that is, every member of the organization exercises leadership from time to time (the definition of leadership being the ability to help the members to work on the tasks that are necessary for the well-being of the school). On this basis the best a head can do is not to get in the way of leadership initiatives of other members of the school. In fact, it would be better on balance for heads to think of themselves essentially as followers rather than leaders. One advantage is that it relieves the felt pressure of being always in charge, always the intitiator, always the one who starts things off and keeps them going. 'Sit back and let it all happen,' would be a good motto for it is only possible to believe in it when you believe in the capabilities of your colleagues.

The nature of teams

Leadership is the key to understanding strategic management which is essentially a team activity. The idea of a team is that people come together as equals to pool their talents and as a consequence of their working together the energy in the group is greater than the simple sum of the parts. To be a member of a team you must be subordinate to the team. For some heads this is a problem because they may see a lack of status which they fear to lose if they are not clearly the person in charge.

Often when heads attend courses with other teachers they find it difficult to accept them as equals. Everyone who has worked with mixed groups knows that some heads have to assert themselves (certainly to identify themselves) as heads. It is partly a way of asking not to be treated like everyone else; a defensive move to pre-empt criticism and being found wanting. Such heads find it impossible to work as team members because they always want to be boss and they surround their membership with conditions, not being bound by the same ground rules as others – for instance, by allowing themselves intermittent membership. Yet unless everyone in the team is under the same constraints and duties there can be no team.

> Many school 'teams' are ineffective simply because there is no equality of membership. In dynamic groups there are no predetermined leaders; leadership arises out of the work to be done.

Perhaps this is the most important truth about headship and ignorance of it probably causes more crises of identity than any other factor.

MANAGERIAL DISTANCING

To work most effectively with a school, heads must be able to distance themselves from it. A manager needs a sense of responsibility and dedication to a school as a job to be done not as a self-indulgence. Schools pass through various stages of development which can be broadly described as stages of innovation and consolidation. The personal qualities of management required for each stage are different and therefore they require different kinds of person. A head suitable for the innovation period will not be happy in the consolidation phase and vice versa.

> Any one individual is unlikely to be suited to a given school for more than a certain period – probably about five to seven years because this is the time it takes by and large for each phase to run.

Therefore, it seems unwise to expect one individual to cope equally with two consecutive phases and if they are in post during the 'wrong' phase they will undoubtedly become stressed. Only a few heads will be able to develop along with the organization but the skills and disposition for so doing are rare.

Management and philosophy

Thinking about oneself and the situation in which one is working is the most important managerial activity anyone can engage in. Organizational problems are the consequence of bad thinking and the answers to organizational problems come only by restating and redefining the problems. The basic cause of stress is the effect that a single and inappropriate interpretation of a situation has upon our behaviour and feelings. A rethinking and restatement of the nature of that world changes the problem and with a continuous application of appraisal the problem that began as intractible becomes soluble.

When individuals becomes stressed it is because they are locked into a single view of things which others do not share and the more unrealistic the view the more personally oppressive it becomes. To prevent a view from becoming immutable we need to be open to feedback from others that confirms or disconfirms our view but we cannot be open to the interpretation of other views if we are afraid of other people. Heads who set themselves apart from their colleagues do not hear the information they need and their false views lead to maverick behaviour.

> Much stress can be avoided by thinking more carefully and sharing those thoughts creatively with respected, though not necessarily agreeing, colleagues.

Blaming colleagues

One of the frequent problems of heads who do not give sufficient freedom and support to their colleagues is that they blame their colleagues for failures that may properly be theirs. It is not unknown for senior managers in any kind of organization to refuse to delegate properly and then to deny responsibility when something goes wrong.

Delegation is impossible without trust and the granting of freedom to perform the delegated tasks as the delegate sees fit.

There is a perpetual problem for many heads who feel that they can only delegate if there is the certainty of success. Perhaps it is a hangover from being overcautious with children but many schools really do lack the atmosphere of trust that has to exist in commercial organizations.

There are two issues. One is the extent of personal anxiety on the part of heads who dare not trust their colleagues adequately and the other is the head's ability to cope when let down. Of course, being let down is concomitant with trust since there can be no trust if there is no risk; in trusting anyone we recognize the risk and assess our ability to cope if the colleague fails. Part of that coping must be the supporting of colleagues not the reprimanding of them.

Some heads fear to trust their colleagues with the consequence that their colleagues become less and less able to accept responsibility thus increasing the burden of responsibility on the head.

Ask yourself whether you really want to trust anyone else, or are you afraid of someone else becoming more knowledgeable or more powerful?

Sometimes heads are too protective of their colleagues. Perhaps schools are too protective of their pupils and do not allow them fully the responsibilities they can handle. Certainly schools vary in the general level of risk-taking and protectiveness. Being overprotective creates a burden, too. Heads can become very paternalistic (both men and women heads) especially towards young colleagues. Young teachers may seem little more than sixth formers, and may seem less sure of themselves.

A large school can have something of a family atmosphere about it with all age groups represented in all the adult states – married, single, divorced, gay, childless, etc. If the family concept can be developed it is a positive force for emotional support. But it must be a very open and extended concept of the family and not one in which the head rules over as the patriarch or matriarch.

Being too protective and yet expecting too much can be a destructive experience because no one else can be what we would like them to be. For some heads, being protective is easier than sharing or delegating responsibility.

RELATIONSHIPS OUTSIDE THE SCHOOL

Special interests

There are some areas of concern that fall to the head almost exclusively. One is the relationship with the LEA and HMI, and also the governors. The head has a very particular relationship in these respects because of his or her legal position in the school and the view the LEA takes of the head as boss. This provides the head with a lot of advantages but there are also some snags. Perhaps the chief snag is if heads find themselves in disagreement with the governors (or, but in the first instance less likely, with LEA officers). There have been a number of notorious cases where they have come into headlong collision with governors and LEAs, but many more have difficulties that never reach the newspapers.

Avoid confrontation with people who are able to exercise power over you.

The advice is easily given and not easy to follow especially as conflict often becomes a matter of principle (whether it was originally so or not). The question about confrontation is always 'Why do I chose confrontation and not conciliation?' We always have the choice and what we chose is a consequence of our perception of ourselves and sometimes our inclination to self-destructiveness or pigheadedness. What are the fights that must be fought and what are the ones we chose out of cussedness?

In organizations there are no realistic principles that are not ultimately pragmatic; that is, how to keep the school going with as little disturbance as possible. If we find ourselves constantly confronting others we are probably wanting more from the school than it can cope with. Because schools exist for all their members and have to give some return for membership they can only be successfully managed if they are limited to doing certain things while others are outside their remit.

A head who is in constant conflict with the governors and LEA (that is, both of them not just the one) is probably going beyond what can be tolerated and can only expect some rejection and perhaps reprimand as a consequence.

Concern for staff

Another area of stress for a head is the personal problems of his or her colleagues which have external implications. Occasionally teachers become involved with pupils in circumstances that require very delicate handling but teachers have the same problems as other adults in their daily lives. Schools in practice exhibit the same social characteristics of other organizations, even if it is sometimes pretended they are more exemplary. Schools are no more highly 'moral' than are other kinds of organization. Teachers do have divorces, engage in adulterous relationships, embezzle funds, steal from shops, sexually assault children and have incestuous relationships, with the same degree of incidence as society at large, so far as anyone can judge. Teachers experience the same domestic and personal tragedies as anyone else – death, injury, illness, financial disaster.

Whenever such personal problems surface, heads have to deal with them directly, however distressing, and however well they may be prepared for the circumstance. In some ways, heads are called upon to fulfil some of the functions of a minister of religion. They will at one time or another have to visit a bereaved spouse and perhaps several times in a career to visit grieving parents. Coming on top of the many other day-to-day pastoral concerns these events can be very distressing and very demanding. Heads require a great deal of help in the pastoral aspects of their job and this is the most neglected area of all in head-teacher training and support.

BEING YOURSELF AND SUSTAINING YOURSELF

Personal realism

In the end, our ability to deal with and even cope with the problems of being boss depends on the realism with which we understand ourselves. One of the first things heads realize when they take up their first headship is that they do not feel any different. Many heads respond to their new job by trying to act out what they believe to be the appropriate behaviour for a head. They role-play in terms of their private stereotype; and they physically dress the part by wearing the kinds of clothes they think heads ought to wear. Not many heads wear jeans even when some of their staff do!

But such role-playing is a potentially stressful activity when the role does not come naturally − and even when it does there may be problems of self-deception. The fact is we cannot sustain a role based on what we believe we ought to be when our natural disposition draws in another direction.

> Heads who cope well choose to 'be themselves' in the position knowing that in this way they have greatest control over their behaviour and feelings. Trying to be what you are not is a recipe for disaster.

Successful managers do those things they know they do best and then find others to do the things they cannot do well.

So really, the self-image of the head is paramount. There are, of course, no 'correct' ways of being a head that can be determined from without the school. There is only the seeking of the best match between what you are and what you have to do. A realistic self-image means that you have a good idea of your strengths and weaknesses, are not over-confident or too diffident, that you do not have a high opinion of your status and, more than anything else, that you do not take yourself too seriously. Unless you can, and do, laugh at yourself you will become unbearably stuffy.

Heads tend to expect too much of themselves and when they gather together they reinforce this expectation. Perhaps many heads are over-achievers, certainly some seem to seek continual justification. Some work too hard at activities external to the school; some neglect the school in their quest for confirmation by colleagues; some hide away from their incompetence by always being engaged elsewhere in or out of the school. In the end, a head must face up to the school in terms of being only one resource person among many and set about helping others to fulfil themselves so that the tasks of the school are equitably shared.

Pacing to avoid stress

Everyone has to understand how we create meaning for ourselves in what we do and to acknowledge the significance timing has in our lives. For instance, some people are never late for a meeting while other are always late. We all of us have certain behaviour patterns that are predictable and characteristic. We each have certain pacings that characterize the way we do things, that are unique to us and may be at odds with other people's. For example, some people are good at producing reports or discussion papers which they do with great facility. Others make very good verbal critiques of them while never actually writing anything down. Yet others are good at producing a second draft with second thoughts and they only do this after the first paper has been discussed. Such reactions are all part of our normal work pacing; some of us get to it at once, others at the last minute; some with great attention to detail and much research, others with broad conceptualization. Some heads prepare for assemblies with great deliberation while others extemporize on topics they think of on the way from their study. Without clear understanding of our own pacing we will never be able to come to terms with the demands of any job we are given.

If we don't understand how we pace ourselves we may panic too often or withdraw simply because we have not been able to accept that our own way is legitimate so long as it works for us.

External support

Quite probably heads seek the support of other heads far too much. They are often observed in defensive groupings and when they meet together ostensibly for moral support the effect is often one of exacerbating personal stress because heads talk about schools and their own behaviour in highly normative ways. It is very difficult for a head to ask for help on very personal and professional matters let alone matters of intimacy. The greatest fear of a head (as of a teacher in the classroom) is any admission that they may not be coping. Yet large numbers of heads do feel that they are not coping and they certainly do not receive the help they need.

By meeting with other heads, they confirm their own way of looking at the world and become closed to other ways of seeing it. There are enormous pressures on schools to be alike. There is much talk of 'good practice' as if it were a universal verity and many assumptions about a 'best' way even when it is hinted that there may be others. The mere fact that alternatives are spoken of so cautiously indicates that there are doubts whether alternatives are quite proper. It is imperative for heads to seek the company of managers from other professions – and not just members of Rotary or the Freemasons.

Management in education has been remarkable for its continued separation from other forms of management – business, commerce, industry, public service. Perhaps heads feel at a disadvantage that they do not speak the same language and have a fear that they are not interested enough in commercial considerations. The fact is that management ideas are universal and not only will heads learn a lot from industry but industry has a great deal to learn from education; certainly businessmen could be helped to understand better the problems of schools for they do not have the same singularity of purpose that most small businesses have.

Counselling and co-counselling

It is useful for heads from time to time to undertake a course of personal 'therapy' – limbering up for emotional fitness. Of course, teachers would benefit, too, by so doing but for heads it is most important. You cannot deal with other people's problems unless you understand your own. Heads can be too eager to offer help because of their own hang ups rather than out of their own emotional well-being. Everyone finds it useful from time to time to take a course of self-examination and to learn the creative skills of introspection. Some heads find that one of the various courses of counselling training are helpful and there is little doubt that counselling skills are the most useful of all management skills. Heads should take time out to reflect under guidance and in a learning group on their behaviour, perceptions and understandings.

For many heads a programme of co-counselling with a non-teaching friend would be very helpful indeed. Schools are miniature worlds and a never-ending emotional challenge; new issues and opportunities arise all the time and heads need to be prepared for them. Sometimes the new needs are quite shocking – the recent concern with child sexual abuse is an example. Only a head with ideas well-sorted out would be able to cope with the caring and teaching required in a school in order to deal with such matters. Yet many heads have their own boundaries of acceptability too tightly drawn for them to be able to respond usefully in the school.

Senior management requires considerable openness of mind if it is to cope with the varieties of expectation and viewpoints even among the teaching staff of the school. Some company directors employ a personal consultant with whom they can talk over all manner of problems and issues. The less the consultant knows about the business the better because one of his or her functions is to provide objectivity. Heads could usefully adopt this practice because it will be a long time before schools become organized in a truly collegial fashion. Even if heads do not wish to be isolated, their staff may insist that they are.

FURTHER READING

Acres, David (1984) *Exams without Anxiety*, Deanhouse, Stoke-on-Trent.
Carr, J. L. (1984) *The Harpole Report*, Penguin, Harmondsworth.
Consumers' Association (1982) *Living with Stress*, Consumers' Association, London.
Cottler, S. B. and Guerra, J. J. (1976) *Assertion Training Series: a guide to self-dignity*, Research Press Inc., Champaign, Illinois.
Dalin, Per, Rust, Val and Sumner, Ray (1980) *School Development Guide*, IMTEC/NFER, Windsor.
Dickson, Anne (1982) *A Woman in Your Own Right*, Quartet, London.
Everard, K. B. and Morris, Geoffrey (1985) *Effective School Management*, Harper & Row, London.
Gray, H. L. (1985) *Change and Management in Schools*, Deanhouse, Stoke-on-Trent.
Handy, Charles and Aitken, Robert (1986) *Understanding Schools as Organizations*, Penguin, Harmondsworth.
Heller, Mary Brownscombe (1983) *Coping with Stress*, Springfield Cooperative Enterprises, Teeside.
Murgatroyd, Stephen (1986) *Counselling and Help*, Methuen, London.
Prather, Hugh (1970) *Notes to Myself*, Real People Press, Moab, Utah.

INDEX